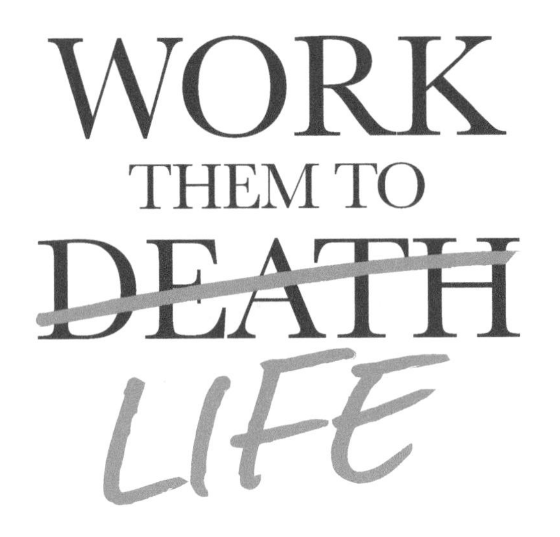
WORK
THEM TO
DEATH
LIFE

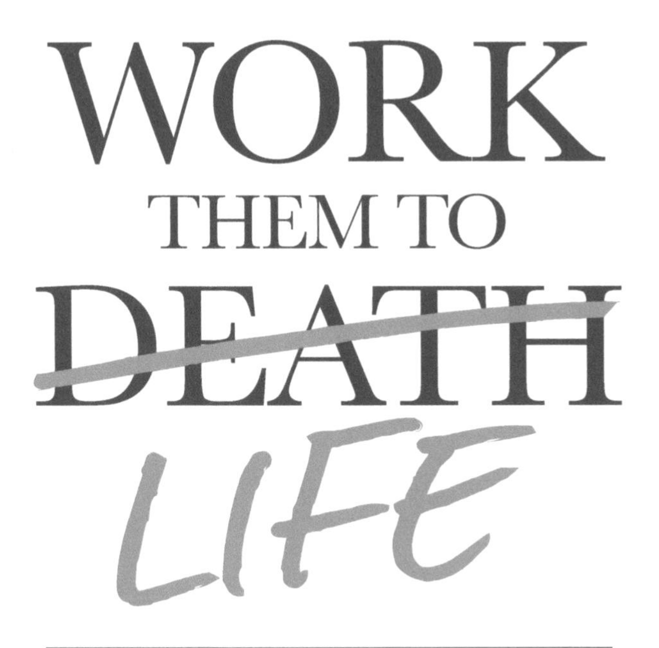

UPGRADE YOUR OFFICE SPACE TO WIN THE TALENT WAR

JIM SCALO

First Printing: 2018

ISBN: 978-0-692-16227-9

The front cover features a rendering of The Riviera, a forthcoming dynamic office space from Burns Scalo Real Estate. Architectural design of the Riviera by NEXT Architecture of Pittsburgh, PA.

For my wife,
who taught me that in the end,
the only thing worth being remembered for
is kindness.

CONTENTS

CONTENTS

ACKNOWLEDGEMENTS

To adequately thank all the people who have made this book possible would be an unachievable task. Over the years, I have observed and learned from many individuals whose wisdom enhances these pages. Life is about "the thick, the thin, and the thick," I often joke, and I am grateful to everyone who has influenced me.

Specifically, I am grateful to my wife and children. Having two girls and two boys has taught me much about DNA—mainly that we are all unique and evolving.

My deepest thanks to my longtime assistant Anissa Eckert, who we call "AAA," for "Always Ask Anissa." Thank you to the entire staff at BSRE, who always faithfully listen to me preach and teach and then repeat. To Chris Flickinger, thank you for providing development and life skills to our organization and myself, and for introducing me to the idea of writing a book.

Thank you to all the contributors who shared their insight and experience in the interview segments of this book. Special thanks to Mandy Stoffel, who designed the cover and creative graphics throughout these pages. Lastly, thank you to Kyle Fager, my book consultant, or ghostwriter, who already has me thinking of my second book.

AUTHOR'S NOTE

My leap of faith to write this book stemmed from the desire to educate occupiers and brokers on an evolving paradigm in the commercial real estate industry. While this book's focus is on professional office space, it certainly relates to all real estate product types.

This is because, in the end, the message isn't about the real estate at all. It's about the people. Call it social psychology if you'd like, but it stems from the simple fact that all businesses are about two things: People and Money. If you want to make more money, then you need the best people (and more of them). Real estate is a necessary part of the secret sauce of success in that endeavor.

If you want to reach the best people, then you start by figuring out what they want, and these days, what they want might surprise you. I can't believe how fast our society is moving and changing—not only in terms of technology, but also in terms of lifestyle. The world has flattened, and the pace of change is rapid. Human conduct is now live and in the moment.

At the time of this writing, unemployment has dipped below 4%, which means that the best talent has more choices about where to work. Additionally, the workforce is quickly becoming younger, and younger generations have overwhelmingly shown that they demand luxury and convenience in their workplaces. Like it or not, this is the new reality.

For all these reasons, your office is no longer just a place to house your employees; it is also a positive weapon to win the talent war. It is a powerful supplemental tool for recruitment, retention, reduction in absenteeism, and ultimately, an improvement in productivity.

My view is that with sincere leadership, a strong culture, and great real estate in the right location, your business will thrive and win the future, while those businesses that don't follow this movement will lose market share.

I believe so much in this future that I didn't just write a book about it; I'm also putting my money where my mouth is and constructing a $35 million riverfront office complex on speculation. You've seen that complex, the Riviera, on the cover of this book. You will see more of it, along with many other inspiring office spaces, in the pages to come.

For more information, please visit www.workthemtolife.com.

BUILDING A

BUILDING B

CHAPTER 1

ALL BUSINESSES ARE ABOUT TWO THINGS

Let's start simple. To the left, you see a series of pictures depicting two very different office spaces. Where would *you* rather work?

Imagine spending your day on a pair of job interviews with competing companies. Since you're a highly talented professional, either of these employers would be thrilled to have you. Your first interview takes place in Building A. Low ceilings. Narrow hallways. Tight elevators. Boxy offices with tiny windows. A drab break room. Ultimately, you decide that you're willing to overlook all of it because of the great salary and benefits. The job just feels like a perfect fit. For now, you're planning to accept the offer.

But then comes your next interview. When you get your first look through the glass front door of Building B, your immediate reaction is *wow.* You've heard and read about offices this amazing, but until this moment, you'd never imagined yourself having the chance to actually *work* in one. You're standing on a beautiful concrete patio lined with café tables and potted plants. There's soft music playing, and it carries you into a sleek, impressive lobby of glass and vibrant color. Inside, you're greeted by the inviting scent of fresh coffee. There's what looks like a concierge desk in the center of the room. You see lounge seating and tables occupied by coworkers who seem genuinely happy to be here. In one corner is a café. In another corner, there's a small group discussing a project while playing shuffleboard. Behind a glass wall to your right, there's a fitness center busy with coworkers exercising in the middle of the day.

This is not the vibe of a workplace. This is the vibe of somewhere you would actually *enjoy* spending time. Even before you get on the elevator, you can see yourself working here. More importantly, you can envision how a space like this would make certain aspects of your personal and professional life more convenient. This convenience will help you meet your needs more efficiently, which will in turn allow you to work harder

---

Opposite: Architectural design of Building B by NEXT Architecture.

while you're in the office. Now you're not just excited about the job you've come to interview for; you're excited about the *life* you might have a chance to lead here.

Upstairs, the office space is like the perfect continuation of the lobby—bright, modern, and exciting. The architecture is inspiring, the flow of work is open and collaborative, and everyone seems to enjoy being around each other. Even though it's a late afternoon in October, natural light floods the room. The air is fresh and clean smelling. The amenities are as nice and as numerous as any luxury hotel. The café is prettier than the kitchen you just finished remodeling at home. And you still can't take your mind off that *fitness center* on the first floor.

There's no question where you'd rather work. You sign with the second company because they're not just offering you a job; they're offering a dramatic improvement to your *lifestyle*, and you can see yourself thriving here.

Now let's flip the script. You're that second employer, the one with the space and amenities that inspired the talented new hire to accept your job offer. Sure, you had to make the investment to create this amazing space, and the rent is higher, but look what just happened. You just won a key battle in the ongoing talent war—a war that, thanks to some troubling demographic trends, is only going to continue its escalation in the near future.

Technology companies were the first to see the growing talent gap on the horizon, but the best and brightest companies in the world—companies of every size and from every industry—have started joining the revolution. They're setting in motion plans to move to better, more attractive office space today, so that by tomorrow, they have an advantage that will win them the loyalty and productivity of the best people in the workforce.

So, where do you house your company? If you're still in Building A, it's time to either embrace a new line of thinking about your office space or get ready for a *brutal* ten-year run. Conversely, if you're in Building B, now you have a new employee with the exact skills you need to keep your company growing. And he won't be the last great candidate you successfully recruit and retain long-term, either, because he and everyone else who joins him will be genuinely happy working here. They will give you exceptional loyalty, great production, and likely a whole lot of innovative thinking. They might even give you all that at a salary lower than the competition was offering.

And that's just the *recruitment* part of the show. Winning these kinds of battles also gives you competitive advantage in a host of ways that might not be immediately apparent.

PEOPLE AND MONEY

As the title for this chapter suggests, all businesses—no matter what their backgrounds—are about two things: people and money. Get better **people,** take good care of them, make more **money**. Everyone understands that. But what the smartest business leaders recognize is that the place where you work is so much more than just a place to house your people. It contributes to your culture. It influences employee loyalty. It connects your business to the community and your clients. It plays a major role in recruitment, retention, and productivity. And ultimately, all these components combine to significantly impact your bottom line and align your business with continued growth for many years to come.

The effect is similar to Jim Collins's excellent analogy in *Good to Great*: the best business leaders don't just tell their employees to get on the bus so they can drive them to the destination. Rather, "They start by getting the right people on the bus, the wrong people off the bus, and the right people in the right seats."[1]

With your office space, the goal should be to put the right people in the right space with the right location and the right culture. That's exactly what this book is all about. Right people, right space, right location, right culture, right leadership. Get these five components in alignment, and not only will you win the talent war, but your top talent will thrive, and your business will thrive, as well.

---

1 Collins, Jim. *Good to Great: Why Some Companies Make the Leap and Others Don't.* HarperBusiness, 2001.

THE NEXT COMPETITIVE ADVANTAGE

As a business leader, you are likely to have spent huge amounts of time and energy looking for competitive advantage. You've reshaped strategies, tightened up your marketing and messaging, and invested in your intellectual property. These are important paths to pursue, of course, but the unfortunate reality is that competitive advantages in these areas don't last as long as they used to. That thing that makes you different? As soon as the competition gets hold of it, or as soon as technology changes enough to disrupt your strategy, that thing becomes obsolete.

Upgrading your office space changes the game on competitive advantage partly because it's *tangible.* Unlike a messaging, IP, or software upgrade, you can actually see, touch, and interact with an office in the real world. As far as competitive advantages go—particularly in the talent war—this is the most high-impact way to enhance how people perceive your business, but more importantly, how they *physically* and *emotionally* interact with it.

Don't underestimate the power of tangibility. If you provide a uniquely compelling, beautiful, engaging place to work, it's next to impossible for the competition to *copy* it. But more importantly—as the best companies we work with at Burns Scalo Real Estate have shown time and time again—decision-makers in every industry are *overlooking* the competitive advantage that is exceptional office space. What this means is that while the wave among the best companies is already happening, it's not too late for you to catch it, to get ahead of it, and to ride it to a brighter future. This is the next major competitive advantage, and that's partly because so many business leaders are ignoring it.

If you make this leap, you will enjoy a strong competitive advantage not just in recruiting, but *across the board.* Think about retention, for example. In the next chapter, we're going to get into the startling numbers behind what employee turnover is costing you, but for now, let's just think about the savings of retaining your top employees.

Those amazing amenities and services you offer in your office space aren't just going to attract new recruits; they're going to *retain* your best people, as well. Leaving one job for a comparable job is easy, especially if it comes with an increase in salary or some other benefit. But if you have to think about leaving not just your job, but also the fitness center you use four afternoons a week, that café that serves the awesome breakfast smoothie you enjoy every morning, the second-to-none coffeemaker that jumpstarts every day, the concierge service that will handle your dry cleaning and get your shoes shined, and that on-floor laundry room you can't imagine your life without, then the choice to leave gets that much tougher to justify. You're not just leaving a job anymore; you're leaving a *lifestyle* that offers a host of services you've gotten addicted to.

The choice gets tougher still when you think about all the close bonds you've made with your coworkers—bonds that have formed from all the cross-talk and meet-by-accident situations that happen naturally in more modern, open, and collaborative office environments. Now, you're not just thinking about leaving your coworkers and joining some new ones; now you're mulling the prospect of having to leave the *friends* you join for lunch every day in the café, your *friends* from the at-work ping-pong league, your *friends* who motivate you every day to stay fit and eat well, and your *friends* from the many social gatherings made possible in that dynamic office space. You're not just leaving a job anymore; you're leaving your most reliable (and your favorite) social circle.

Even if the money or opportunity might be slightly better with that other employer, why in the world would you want to leave?

So here you are as an employer enjoying the next major competitive advantage. You're winning the war for top talent and you're retaining your best employees. All those luxurious amenities you're offering will also make those employees *want* to be at work more often. Absenteeism will drop. Productivity will soar. Your company will be able to do more than it ever could before, all because your people haven't just found a work/life balance, but a work-life *blend.*

BLEND VS. BALANCE

Every other company in your market is looking for ways to allow their employees better work/life balance. They're moving to flex hours, trying to soften their stances on how people manage their personal lives, and even letting them work from home or otherwise remotely. These are fine principles, but everybody's doing them. What's more, studies show that most employees are less productive and more detached from the culture and identity of the company when they spend more time working remotely.

The other problem with *balance,* as pointed out in Dan Thurmon's brilliant *Off Balance on Purpose: Embrace Uncertainty and Create a Life You Love,*[2] is that it's not just unachievable, but *undesirable,* as well. If you're trying to *balance* your personal life with your work life, then certain elements of one always have to offset certain elements of the other. It's a give and take situation. With work-life *blend,* however, you're forgetting about trying to achieve balance between your work product, professional aspirations, friendships, health and wellness, and entertainment, and instead you're *blending* those elements together into the ideal day to day existence. Now you don't have to think of things in terms of spaces where you do your work and drudge through what you "have to do" compared with spaces where you can relax and "be yourself." Now a blend of work and life happens in the office even as that same blend follows you home. Meanwhile, you can do what you have to do while being yourself both at home and the office.

As an employer, if you can provide the opportunity for work-life blend, the results are nothing short of magic. You transform your office space from just another place to work into a *vibrant and collaborative community.* Of course, getting there starts with leadership, but your office space is a **powerful supplemental tool** to help your people meet more of their needs, feel a heightened sense of belonging, and create that communal culture that leads to such a positive, collaborative, and productive environment. I used the word "magic," but really, it's all a matter of *logic.* If you offer a beautiful café with healthy food, then your people are more likely to interact, socialize, and collaborate with each other during the early morning and at lunch instead of leaving the building. If you have a fitness center, then your people get all those same communal benefits while they're simultaneously meeting an important health need—additionally, they're likely to be less inclined to cut out early so they can beat the rush at the fitness mega-center up the street.

---

2 Thurmon, Dan. *Off Balance on Purpose: Embrace Uncertainty and Create a Life You Love*. Motivation Works, Inc., 2016.

It's a simple concept: if your office space helps your people meet the need to socialize, then the sense of community and belonging improves, and everyone starts *wanting* to spend more time in the office. And as a giant added benefit, people who eat healthier, exercise regularly, and enjoy a positive social life are substantially happier, and as a result, far more productive. By the way, this isn't something that just benefits your people, either; their happiness also shows to your customers. That's the powerful supplemental tool in action: a relatively minor investment in improving your office space leads to an improved work-life blend for your people, a better relationship with your customers, and a *giant* improvement to your bottom line.

EVOLVE OR GO EXTINCT

Let me clear up a quick potential misconception: while I do believe that *new* buildings housing *new* office space are the best play for your next office move, I am by no means suggesting that what you might describe as an *old* building is always obsolete. An old building can deliver all these same competitive advantages. It's just that it usually must be gutted and completely renovated to meet the exacting standards we'll be covering in this book.

It's very important to remember that I'm not advocating putting lipstick on pigs. You can't just set up a ping-pong table and expect it to change things on its own. Whether you're weighing a move into a new building or the renovation of an old one, the important thing to think about is how to meet as many needs as possible for the people who make you money. After all, demographics are shifting, those people are going to be changing, and so are their needs. So why wouldn't you change along with them?

The future of office space is one that sees offices constructed with sustainable materials, the best technology, and the best amenities. Efficient glass, great lighting that mimics natural light patterns, clean and fresh-smelling air. Bigger floors that fit more people, bigger restrooms, bigger elevators. Exceptional amenities inside and outside the building, and exceptional services to supplement them. We'll meet soaring demand for all that electricity to serve all that advancing technology with sustainable sources. More employers will begin thinking about how nutrition, exercise, and value-added services can improve their employees' health and general sense of wellbeing, and in turn, their productivity. When they do this, their office space will speak loudly not just about how much they care about their employees, but about who they are as a company.

So what does your office space say about your company? What kind of message does it send to your people, to your recruits, to your clients, and to your community? Believe me, it's saying more than you realize. So wouldn't it be better if the message was overwhelmingly positive?

It has been widely reported that today's top companies have already invested in this concept. All that wealth churning around in the S&P 500 seems to flow disproportionately toward the Googles and Apples and Facebooks of the world. And that disproportionate flow is happening for a hugely important reason: those top companies have made substantial effort to improve not just the spaces where their employees work, but everything about those employees' lifestyles.

The evolution of office space at Google has transformed work into something much more than just work. Google's sprawling campus is also a place to collaborate, a place to innovate, a place to eat, a place to exercise and do your laundry, a place to play, and a place to genuinely enjoy spending time. The result? Google (and any other company that shares their thinking on work-life blend) has no trouble recruiting the world's most talented people. And those world's-most-talented-people will ensure that Google will remain one of the most powerful and profitable companies on the planet. They will always get better people, and they will always treat them better than other companies, so they will always make more money.

The case for higher quality office space seems simple when you look at it that way. But the trouble is that too many decision-makers still trip up on three common objections: 1) I don't run a technology company like Google, so what does this have to do with me? 2) This sounds like a Millennial thing, and 3) the rent is too high. Let's cross out those objections, one by one.

BUT I DON'T RUN A TECHNOLOGY COMPANY...

Okay, so your company isn't a big tech firm. But this sea change toward inspiring office space with more attractive amenities and a better work-life blend is absolutely *not* just for Google, Apple, and Facebook. Yes, the movement was begun by (mostly) technology companies, but just because they were at the forefront of seeing this strategy as effective in the talent war, that doesn't mean they're alone. Companies across all spectrums of business and in every industry are slowly beginning to adapt to the model. It doesn't matter if you're small, mid-sized, or large, either; you can and will see benefits from following Big-Tech's lead toward dynamic office space.

In the pages to come, we're going to be taking a look at some firsthand perspectives on exactly this point, and we'll draw them from some of the best companies we have ever worked with at Burns Scalo. We'll examine three very different organizations: one small, one mid-sized, and one large.

For the first category, we will follow the story of Blattner Brunner, Inc., a once-small marketing firm whose pioneering approach to dynamic office space helped it grow into a mid-sized company that occupies the top spot in its market.

In the mid-sized category, we'll examine the exceptional returns of a recent move into a beautiful new office building by Waldron Private Wealth, a nationally recognized and locally acclaimed financial services firm that also happens to be consistently rated as one of Pittsburgh's best places to work.

And for the large category, we'll check in with Rice Energy, cited as one of the fastest growing companies in America just prior to its recent acquisition by energy giant EQT. The Rice Energy story is particularly illuminating in that they began as a startup before a meteoric climb to the top of a booming industry, an IPO, and a highly lucrative sale. Along the way, they embraced the stabilizing power that exceptional amenities and beautiful space can add to a talented, rapidly growing staff.

All three of these companies realized success in part because they asked themselves the same question that most Big-Tech firms like Google asked a long time ago: What does it take to grow? To find the answer, let's picture a modern startup. What do we know about them? They're small, they don't have a ton of market share, and they're running on a shoestring. But when you think about a modern startup, what kind of office space do you picture? Yes, there are the stories of some companies starting in a garage (Google and Apple are among them), but let's move past that point and imagine what it looks like after they finally get to where they need office space. What does that space look like?

The answer is simple: it looks pretty cool. The environment is probably open, with lots of engaged, inspired people collaborating and innovating together. The leader of this company has probably taken great care to make sure everyone is as healthy and happy and comfortable as possible. There's a nice café. Shared workspaces. A slick, modern conference room or two. Plenty of natural light. There's probably a ping-pong table somewhere.

Here's the reason we all picture roughly the same thing: startups that wind up achieving success pretty much all get there for the same reasons. They worked hard and rode their innovations toward rapid and sustained growth. To do that, they needed hard-working and innovative people. They attracted those hard-working and innovative people not with high salaries and great benefits (because while they were startups, they couldn't afford them), but with the kinds of spaces that ensure a more attractive work-life blend. Those spaces also ensured that the startup's top minds remained stimulated, creative, inspired, invested, and working hard. In short, those funky little spaces aren't a side-effect of modern startups; they're a *driver* of their success. They are evidence of a disruption of commercial office space—a disruption that only the world's best business leaders, no matter what size their companies, are taking advantage of.

And one more point about this first objection: Do you *really* think you're not in the technology business? My company, Burns Scalo, invests in commercial real estate. The three companies we'll be checking in on throughout this book do marketing, financial advisory, and energy, respectively. None of them are "technology companies." And many of the companies on the S&P 500 that are currently engaged with moving their home offices to dynamic new spaces are also not "technology companies." But what happens at any of these companies when the email system goes down? What happens at your company when you lose your WiFi? Everything grinds to a halt, right? Think about the last time you sat in on a presentation where the projection system didn't work. How'd that one go? How long did it take to get the meeting started?

We can't do *anything* without the technology we rely on to get our jobs done. There was a time when we "went" to the Internet. Now we do *all* our work there. Now we *live* on it. What this means is that *all of us*—every last one of us in a business leadership role—runs or works for a technology company, whether we like to admit it or not. And as the years go by, and more and more of our staff is made up of younger generations, the lines of distinction are only going to get blurrier.

So, yes, when you hear about these things, it's mostly from the Googles of the world. But there's a reason so many people want to work at Google. People used to think about these amenities as a fad or a joke, but they are neither. They are the *reason* Google is getting the most talented people and dominating their market.

In your own market, if there isn't currently a company with a Google-like space, then there will be soon. Not long after, the spaces and practices discussed in this book will become mainstream. What's that old adage again—the one about the benefits of being first to market? The question isn't whether you *can* afford to lead this sea change toward better office space. The question is whether you can afford *not to.* And as we'll see shortly, the difference in cost isn't in any way significant. We're not talking about spending huge amounts of money that you weren't going to spend already. We're talking about the delta—the small difference in the rent you pay now between the rent you would have to pay to occupy a dynamic space. When you break it down in terms of a percentage of your overall operating budget, the switch to a better space becomes a no-brainer.

THIS SOUNDS LIKE A MILLENNIAL THING…

Luxury, quality, lifestyle, sustainability—these are the kinds of things Millennials are always talking about. Why should I focus on it when it has always been true that success comes from saving money, keeping your head down, and working harder than the competition?

There are two problems with this line of thinking. First, it assumes that the generations that occupy your workforce will remain static. Yes, today's workforce includes a small number of people from the Silent Generation (anyone born between 1933 and 1945) and a larger but rapidly dwindling number of Baby Boomers (born between 1946 and 1966). Many people currently occupying leadership roles hail from Generation X (born between 1967 and 1981), but more and more of those roles are starting to go to Millennials (1982-1995). And if you can believe it, Generation Z (1996-present day) is also starting to enter the workforce.

Now, under no circumstances is this going to be another book about Millennials.[3] And I won't get into the existential dread I feel when I think about the fact that Generation Z has grown up with *no memory* of a world without a ubiquitous Internet and always-connected technology. But this *is* a book that recognizes the reality that the youngest two generations that occupy today's workforce will soon *dominate* that workforce.

Not long from now, Millennials and Generation Z will make up *75%* of the workforce.[4] By then, the companies standing at the top of their industries will be the ones that manage to recruit and retain the most talented people from these two generations. So if you want to think about Millennial preferences as a passing fad, that's your prerogative, but you do so at your company's peril. Millennial preferences aren't going to change. The generation isn't going to "grow up" and work the way we used to work or our parents and grandparents used to work. They're simply going to inherit the decision-making roles, and then their preferences will become the new reality. And if, by then, such a huge

---

3 I don't know about you, but I've gotten pretty tired of books about Millennials.

4 Donston-Miller, Debra. "Workforce 2020: What You Need to Know Now." Forbes.com. May 5, 2016.

percentage of the labor pool is going to be demanding better space and amenities, then you can't afford to *not* make the investment, or all those talented people will go elsewhere.

The other factor at play here is that this is absolutely *not* just a Millennial thing. I don't care what generation you're from—Generation Z, Y, or X, Boomer or Silent or Greatest—if given the choice, you're going to pick Building B over Building A, and you're going to pick it eight days a week. And you're going to do this for the same reason you choose one home over another or one hotel over another. If the difference between luxury and mediocrity is only the delta—that small percentage of a small percentage of your operating budget—then you're going to choose luxury every time.

It doesn't matter where you come from or how old you are, *everyone* would prefer to work in a nicer building. Whatever your thoughts on sit-stand desks and free bananas, it isn't only Millennials whose productivity improves as a result of more positive and healthy environments. Whether you're an Internet-focused, altruistic, pampered Millennial; or you're a tech-savvy, risk-taking, and skeptical Gen Xer; or you're an independent, hard-working, achievement-focused Boomer, you're going to care more about an employer who puts you into a great space. And when you care more, you work harder, you work better, you're more collaborative, you innovate more readily, and you make a more positive impact on your employer's bottom line.

YOU JUST WANT ME TO RAISE MY RENT…

This is a key point. And as someone who runs a real estate brokerage, management, and development firm, it's also an important distinction for me to make. I'm not suggesting that what the world needs is for everyone to think about paying higher rent just for the sake of paying higher rent. Rather, I'm suggesting that most people in the decision-making chair are thinking about rent in all the wrong ways. If you start approaching your rent differently, then you also start leveraging a remarkable opportunity for disruptive competitive advantage.

The prevailing belief in business is that lower rent is always better—that if you want a healthy bottom line, then it helps to keep expenses to a minimum. Business leaders often look to that rent number as this terrifying expense they have to try to cut at all costs. And brokers, even though they make a better commission from a higher rent, tend to focus on driving it down so they can get a "win" for their clients. But if you get trapped in that mode of thinking, then you always end up saving a penny at the expense of making a buck.

Here's why: What percentage of your total expenses goes to rent? If you're like most businesses, the answer is somewhere between 3% and 7%. Now, what percentage goes to payroll and payroll-related items like healthcare, retirement benefits, and so on? Depending on what industry you're in, that number probably falls somewhere between 50% and 65%. You might recognize that those latter numbers are considerably higher than the former. So why, as decision-makers, are we paying so much more attention to saving fractions of percentage points on rent when the quality of our buildings plays such a huge role in the productivity we can expect from our staff?

One brilliant measure of this effect comes from JLL, a global commercial real estate services company with its US headquarters in Chicago.[5] JLL's 3-30-300 Rule invites you to imagine a company that's paying $3 per square foot on utilities, $30 per square foot on rent, and $300 per square foot on labor (in the form of payroll and payroll-related expenses). If you step back and look at those expenses, it's clear where companies should be trying to maximize their return. Unfortunately, most companies are still fixated on the wrong numbers.

"The reason most business leaders are still focusing on things like rent and utilities is because the qualitative aspect of the $300 number is harder to quantify," said JC Pelusi, International Director, Corporate Solutions and the Great Lakes Region at JLL. "The quantitative parts are just easier for decision-makers to focus on. Lately, though, you see a trend toward those people focusing more on the productivity that comes from higher quality office space."

As the JLL model shows, a 10% reduction in utility costs can save you 30 cents per square foot, and a 10% reduction in rent saves you $3 per square foot. But those savings are minor compared to the corresponding

5 http://www.us.jll.com/united-states/en-us

10% loss in employee productivity, which costs you *$30* per square foot. A better strategy, it seems, would be to find ways to maximize the value you're getting from the lesser two expenses. If a 30-cent *raise* in cost for utilities leads to better health and wellness for your staff, and a $3 *raise* in rent-per-square-foot leads to a happier and more productive staff, then you're paid back in spades by that $30-per-square-foot return on your investment in labor.

Meanwhile, the data produced by CBRE, the largest commercial real estate services and investment firm in the world, agrees. Sure, rent matters, but not nearly as much as the expense you must commit to your people. According to David Koch, Executive Vice President of the Corporate Advisory Services Group of CBRE's Pittsburgh office, "The cost per square foot is a good metric, and we continue to use it. However, the economic driver now should be the cost of retention of employees. The money, time, and effort that can be lost if the employee is unhappy with the building or facility that they work in is far greater than the price per square foot." Here's a shorthand way to think about all this: your people don't care about what you're paying in rent. Most often, they don't even know what that number is. All they see is the quality of the office space you provide for them. So why try to send the message that you got the best deal on the rent by occupying the lowest quality space? What exactly can you expect from your people if they look around and see all this tangible evidence that you're more concerned about keeping this incredibly minor expense to a minimum than you are about their comfort, happiness, and wellbeing?

THE DIFFERENCE IS THE DELTA

"The delta" is a term you've seen me reference a few times already, so let's take a moment to define it. Here's that definition: if your rent is 3% to 7% of your operating budget, then it's already a drop in the bucket compared to your larger expenses; and no matter what the quality of your current space, upgrading to a better one is only going to cost you the *delta,* a small percentage of that small percentage of your operating budget. Put another way, by upgrading to dynamic office space, you won't be going from rent that is 0% of your operating budget to rent that's 6%; rather, you'll be going from something like 5% to 6%.

Put an even simpler way, we're talking about the difference between $27 per square foot for average, uninspiring space and $33 per square foot for a luxury space. What does a 20% raise in your rent really matter when your rent is already costing you so little relative to your overall operating budget? And if covering that insubstantial delta between the lower rent and the slightly higher one can get you a corresponding 20% boost in employee productivity across the board? How could you pass on that opportunity?

The Bentley: Architectural design by NEXT Architecture.

Rent doesn't matter. The right office space matters. Getting the right people in the right positions so they can give you optimum productivity matters. If you show your people and recruits that you care, *they* will care about the success of your business in new and far more meaningful ways. Where you choose to house your office represents a significant opportunity to leverage a surprisingly small rent expense into a huge gain in employee morale, loyalty, and productivity while simultaneously reducing costly absenteeism and even costlier employee turnover. And all it costs you is that surprisingly small delta between two insignificant percentage points of your overall operating budget.

IT'S NOT ABOUT THE MONEY (IT'S ABOUT THE MONEY)

Back in 1956, when my dad John Scalo was starting a roofing business in Pittsburgh with his friend Duke Burns, success meant working as hard as possible so that you could have enough to be happy when you retire. The two of them did just that, and their hard work paid off in the form of a company they could pass to the next generation of their families. When I first started running Burns Scalo Real Estate Services in 1994, similar principles held true: work hard today so that tomorrow you can be happy. That concept has certainly played a part in our company's growth to the point where we own and manage over five million square feet of office space in the Midwest. But it wasn't until I changed the way I thought about work—or more specifically, about *motivation*—that the true growth began.

Effective productivity doesn't come from a desire to work hard so that you can be happy when your career is over. It comes first from being happy *while* you work. This work-life blend stuff is more than just a soft new way to look at the corporate world. It isn't evidence that Millennials need to grow up and figure out how things are *really* supposed to be. Rather, it's a better, more powerful perspective. If you're happy, you're more productive. You're clearer headed. You're more willing to collaborate. You're better equipped to think about the big picture. You're more likely to seek reward—both for yourself and your company. And you're far more likely to care about the success of your employer.

I've seen it firsthand. We just made an investment on an expensive buildout and moved our company to a gorgeous new building we call "The Bentley." We're paying the highest rent in the sub-market, but the return has been more than worth it.

The building features all the latest trends in workplace architecture and technology. Everywhere you turn, you see an inspiring collaborative space. And yes, we have the beautiful café, the comfortable lounge, and the fitness center. Doing this came at a not insignificant expense. Plus, it raised our rent. But it also connected our office space with our culture. It demonstrated to our people that we have a desire to invest in their health, wellbeing, and happiness at work. The results in recruitment, retention, loyalty, and productivity have been beyond our expectations. Our building shows our people that their leadership cares, and as a result, *they* care more about the company's success. People are happier, prouder, and more motivated to work for us than ever before, and that has improved our capability, our agility in the market, and our bottom line.

As we'll see as we move through the coming pages, the same was true for Blattner Brunner, Inc., Waldron Private Wealth, and Rice Energy. And it was true because they paid attention to something that most companies were overlooking at the time (and continue to overlook today). Come to think of it, it kind of reminds me of that dial on the dashboard that most people pay almost no attention to...

REV UP YOUR RPMs: RECRUITING, PRODUCTIVITY, AND MONEY

Assuming you don't drive a manual transmission vehicle, you're probably like most people in that you almost never look at the tachometer. Some people pay so little attention to it that they don't even know what its numbers *mean*. The tachometer is essentially the dial that tells you how hard your engine is working. The more you press down on the pedal while in a certain gear, the faster the pistons in the engine beat—a measure known as Revolutions Per Minute, or RPMs.

Now, you may have noticed that, throughout this chapter, we've been discussing three key components of business success, components that conveniently fit into that same RPM acronym: Recruiting, Productivity, and Money. And just like the tachometer on your dashboard, most business leaders today—and even brokers and other real estate insiders—aren't paying enough attention to the RPMs. In that desire to get the lowest rent possible for the most space, too many decision-makers are overlooking how dynamic office space can *rev up* a company's RPMs.

In respect of those RPMs, I have divided this book into three sections, each of them complete with three chapters that speak to one of the three components of the RPM model: Recruiting, Productivity, and Money. There are many key strategies and insights to come, but before we move forward, I'll leave you with one final analogy. The engine in a car requires two inputs to run properly: gasoline and oil. If it has those two inputs, then it produces RPMs at an optimal rate. The title of this chapter is that all businesses are about the same two things. Those two things are **people** and **money.** Think of them as the *inputs* into the engine that is your company. Do right by your people and invest a small delta of your rent money in dynamic office space, and your company engine will be humming like never before. You'll **recruit** the top talent in your market, your company's **productivity** will soar, and you'll make more **money** than ever before.

PART 1:
RECRUITING

CHAPTER 2

THE HIGH COST OF LOSING THE BEST PEOPLE

"The best perk is being treated like a human being."
- Anonymous

We opened chapter 1 with a hypothetical example of a highly talented employee having to choose a comparable job offer between two companies with very different office spaces. A similar example applies here as we move on to the costs (both seen and unseen) of recruitment and retention.

Our story starts with Waldron Private Wealth, a nationally recognized and locally acclaimed financial services firm based in Pittsburgh, PA. Sometime before they started showing up on lists as one of the city's best places to work, company founder John Waldron recognized that his staff wasn't operating at peak efficiency. It's tough, after all, to get to peak when half your staff is in one building and the other half is in the building next door. "We had traditional office space," John said. "Nothing was open. Everybody had their own little office with a closed door. The space was an afterthought—just a place to set up and do our work. As long as our computers worked and we had connectivity, we didn't care what the space looked like.

"But once we got to a certain size as a company, we knew we needed to change. We had grown to the point where it just didn't make sense not to build something of our own. It wasn't until we moved into our new building that we realized how under-efficient we'd been."

That new building, a premium space called "The Beacon," changed just about everything for Waldron Private Wealth. Consider, for example, the impression an office like the one on the next page offers to its visitors.

"That's not just a pretty space," John said. "That's an example of how real estate can be a part of your functional budget. We quickly found that our new space wasn't just space; it helps drive our culture, message, and brand. It provides a bolt of highly positive energy throughout the organization. It was a bigger investment than I considered initially, but it has more than paid off. Everything we do has improved because of this building."

The Beacon – Architectural design by Pfaffmann + Associates, exterior photo by Matthew Shuck.

One of those improvements, and perhaps the most tangible, is recruiting. The most recent recruiting win for Waldron Private Wealth was Lynne

Schultz, a highly talented Business Development Coordinator. Lynne spent the first thirty-four years of her career working for a large financial services company in downtown Pittsburgh. The culture and office space at her previous employer were what you might call traditional, and Lynne wasn't aware of how different her work and life could be until she started to look elsewhere.

"It wasn't that I hated it at my old job," Lynne said. "It's just that I was there for a long time, so I had a sense that this was the way things were *supposed* to be."

Then Lynne awoke to a new understanding. She knew that she wanted to finish her career with a company that didn't just pay her; she wanted an employer with a culture that recognized the work-life blend, one that could give her better opportunity to collaborate with her coworkers. But did that company even *exist* in the financial services world? Everywhere she had been, the story seemed the same: financial companies were all about the work and the numbers, so *everyone* practiced the same kind of culture she was thinking about leaving. "I didn't really know where to look," Lynne said. "All I knew was that it wasn't compensation driving me to find another job. I was looking to improve my mental, emotional, and physical wellbeing."

When a friend told her about the beautiful new building at Waldron Private Wealth, she decided to submit her résumé. "I went into the interview and told them that I was interviewing *them* too. Because at that stage in my career, I wasn't just looking for the next job. I was looking for a landing pad." She could tell from the interview, which focused almost entirely on who she was as a person rather than on the accomplishments listed on her résumé, that this company was different. But what really drove the message home was the space.

"When I first saw the Grand Cayman room (the one with the pool table and the bar)," Lynne explained, "I felt like Carrie Bradshaw in the *Sex and the City* movie, where she sees her amazing new penthouse apartment for the first time and says, 'Hello. I live here.' It blew my mind to think that something like this even *existed* in our industry."

Lynne was of course thrilled when she received the offer from Waldron Private Wealth. And now that she works in such an engaging space, and in a culture that puts her wellbeing first, she can't imagine ever going back to her old life. "Everything about the building affects my mood. Emotionally, when you first walk in, the brightness and openness makes you feel refreshed. Physically, the sit/stand workspaces are more comfortable than anything I've ever had before. And the technology here is amazing. You just step into a conference room and you can instantly share with the screen. I really look forward to going to work every day."

When I asked if the Beacon contributed to her pride and sense of belonging at Waldron Private Wealth, she showed me how she keeps pictures of the building on her cell phone. "Are you kidding?" she said. "Look at this place! I just can't believe the way it brought me back to life. I was in a complacent situation for a long time, and I realized that I'd stopped growing professionally. But when I came here, it just opened up my mind, and my whole world. At fifty-four years old, I feel like an adult again. This was a big step for me to reinvent myself this late in my career. But I just feel so rejuvenated in this space and this culture. I'm growing and changing in a positive way."

If your company isn't in the kind of office space that *attracts* top talent like Lynne, then you're also bound to *lose* top talent. As we'll see in the pages to come, those same tools that improve recruitment also improve retention. The more enjoyable and engaging you make the space, and the more opportunities you give your people to be excited about seeing coworkers they actually *like* and want to be around every day, the more likely they are to *stay* with you for years to come.

THE HIDDEN COSTS OF TURNOVER

Employee turnover is a huge problem for most organizations—but it's an even bigger one for those with outdated office space. There was a time when people would stay with one company all their lives. In fact, we have many people like that at Burns Scalo. But times have changed. Millennials and Generation Z simply don't think about work in the same way we do. People change jobs, employers, and even career paths more frequently than ever.

Not only does this lead many organizations to struggle with keeping roles filled and maintaining a fully productive staff; it also costs them money. Those additional recruiting efforts are expensive, after all, as is training and retraining new employees. And when you combine that with the expectation that an outdated office space is going to lead to lesser quality recruits (because all the best ones choose the better spaces), you also have to factor in the cost of underperformance from the person you're training to replace that talented employee (or rapid succession of employees) you just lost.

Worse yet, when you have to commit all this money and time and energy to keeping your staff whole and all your organizational needs met, it can lead to a drain on commitment and morale for those people who are otherwise loyal to your company. How is David, a twenty-year veteran of your firm, supposed to feel good about his job when every other year he has to teach a new recruit how to work with him? Whether he wants to or not, he's going to start wondering about his true purpose with this company, and whether these young recruits are seeing something he's not. It's only natural to be less engaged in a role when you feel this way.

While all this is happening, there is also the potential that technology helps your competition pass you by. As we've discussed already, the integration of disruptive new technologies in office spaces is a tremendous recruiting and culture-reinforcing tool. It also leads to certain tasks or roles to become automated, which can alter workflows and change the expectations for any number of key roles. In an old building, an employee might have to commit to an hour a day on tasks that could otherwise be automated. Then, when he/she makes the leap to that new employer with the luxurious new building, he/she can spend that time on actual work. This makes the employee more engaged with the job, more productive, and happier overall.

Here's the thing: let's ignore the productivity loss here and just focus on the people element; do you think your existing employees don't see how much easier and better their departing coworkers have it at their new jobs? Even if they never speak directly to that outgoing staff member again, they have social media. They read articles. They get the text messages from friends about the amazing working environment. There are plenty of ways to pick up the buzz that made their former coworker leave.

So how long will they hold out before they decide that enough is enough and follow that departing employee out the door? If you're not showing your people that you're willing to make the investment in their contentment with work and their overall work-life blend, then their loyalty will only take you so far.

In summary, generational differences lead to more turnover and a more cutthroat talent war; recruiting, training, and retraining cost money and time; consistent turnover damages morale, saps energy, and shreds productivity for existing employees; and the quality of your office space and technology only drives further turnover.

These are already steep costs, and we haven't even started discussing the cost of losing a key skill. I can't tell you how many companies I've encountered where they do a whole lot of things for a whole lot of people, but when you break it all down, without that one key employee, the entire operation would grind to a halt. What would it cost to lose that person? The straight answer is either "nearly everything" or "everything." This factor is terrifying on a more local level, as well. Even if your organization doesn't rely on a single key player, surely there are teams and projects that would suffer if they lost one or two important contributors.

With the generational drift set to take the talent war to new heights in the coming years, these are no longer problems for the HR department to worry about. Retaining more employees is a business strategy that will directly impact your bottom line. Retaining your people helps avoid the costs of replacing them, but taking strides to make them happier at work also keeps them energized and productive while they're under your employ. In this way, having the kind of building where people actually *enjoy* spending time improves not just retention and engagement, but it enhances *everything* you do as an organization, drives customer satisfaction, and generates higher profits. Better space, lower turnover expenses, more cohesive staff and culture, higher profits—what's not to love about this strategy?

DELTA POINT:
YOUR RENT WILL NEVER BE ZERO

Before we crunch the numbers on what employee turnover is really costing you, let's return to one of the common objections we engaged with in chapter 1. Yes, upgrading to a new and better building full of modern amenities costs money. At first glance, it might seem like you will have to pay a premium to enjoy the many cultural, staffing, and financial benefits of dynamic office space. But again, the truth is that there is not a huge difference in expense. The difference is the delta between the rent you're already paying and the slightly higher rent it takes to occupy one of these awe-inspiring spaces.

Think of it this way: your rent will never be zero dollars. We're not talking about going from rent taking up 0% of your operating budget to 7%. We're talking about going from maybe 5% to 7%. The difference between $27 per square foot for your outdated space and $33 per square foot for a modern, impressive space is negligible—it's the delta, a small percentage of a small percentage.

Actually, let's put it another way. In the real estate industry, we're always getting hung up on price per square foot and percentages. So let's throw that out and discuss real dollars for a moment. Let's say your rent is $120,000 per year for an outdated space. Now let's say that the space that can rev your RPMs and help you win better recruits, get better productivity, and make more money will cost you $144,000. Are we really getting hung up on $24,000? How's that $24,000 going to look when your outdated space starts costing you your best employees?

WHAT IS EMPLOYEE TURNOVER REALLY COSTING YOU?

Let's imagine that you have 100 employees. If you spend the next ten years in an outdated building, you're likely to see higher-than-average turnover. This is because every year that you throw band-aids over the problems your space is causing, you'll see more and more of your valuable employees leave for other jobs in better spaces. But just for the sake of argument, let's say that you somehow manage to convince the average number of them to stay despite the allure of those more attractive office spaces. This means that you will experience exactly the current national average of employee turnover, or 18.5% of your people every year (another scary factor is that the percentage gets higher every year, but for the sake of this hypothetical, we'll ignore that troubling trendline).

So every year for ten years, you're going to have to say goodbye to 18.5% of your people and then train and outfit their replacements. According to Jack Altman, CEO of Lattice, the cost for each replacement follows this formula:[1]

Hiring
+ Onboarding
+ Development
+ Unfilled Time
x Number of Employees
x Annual Turnover Percentage

= Annual Cost of Turnover

Feel free to plug those into a spreadsheet to find your own (harrowing) number, but for now, let's stick to the averages. According to Altman, the average company spends $25,000 to hire someone new and $10,000 on the turnover and development process, and then there is the productivity loss to the tune of another $50,000. That's $85,000 for the average employee, for those scoring at home. Multiply that by the 100 employees

1 Altman, Jack. "How Much Does Employee Turnover Really Cost?" Huffington Post. January 18, 2017.

in your company, and the 18.5% turnover rate is going to cost you nearly $1.6 million. *Annually*. That's $16 million over the next ten years.

This is only the beginning too. That $16 million figure is only relevant if you manage to replace each departing employee with *exactly* the right person, and you do so *immediately*. If you've ever had to fill a vacant role, you know that this doesn't always happen. In fact, according to the National Federation of Independent Businesses, 60% of employers suffer through job openings that stay vacant for more than twelve weeks.[2] Twelve weeks! How much productivity are you losing when a key job remains unoccupied for a full fiscal quarter? What's this doing to your revenues? And how is this affecting your customers, who have to go without that missing employee with whom they've built a relationship?

At Burns Scalo, we recently changed our IT providers because the people we liked from that firm left for another one. We liked those people so much that we moved our account *with* them. So how many accounts are you losing when your people depart for another company?

And all this is just for the *average* employee. Yes, it's less costly to replace lower-paying jobs (those working for hourly wages or earning under $30,000 per year tend to cost only $3,300 to replace, while those making between $30,000 and $50,000 check in around $20,000 each[3]), but what if the next ten years leads to more turnover in the management and executive tiers of your company? Replacing a highly educated contributor costs up to a staggering 213% of that person's annual salary.[4] If we imagine their salaries as a nice, round $100,000, then that's $213,000 per loss at the upper management level. You don't have to lose too many of these people for the costs to get untenable.

---

2 Schawbel, Dan. "10 Workplace Trends You'll See In 2018." Forbes.com. November 1, 2017.

3 Lucas, Suzanne. "How Much Does It Cost Companies to Lose Employees?" CBS News. November 21, 2012.

4 Merhar, Christina. "Employee Retention – The Real Cost of Losing an Employee." Peoplekeep.com. February 4, 2016.

DON'T FORGET THE COST OF ABSENTEEISM

Turnover is terrifyingly expensive, but the startling truth is that the subject covers only the *longer-term* losses in productivity that an outdated, uninspiring building can cause. Every day, there's a chance that one of your people might not arrive for work. Whether they're sick, distracted by something at home, or they just don't feel like coming in today for one reason or another, absenteeism costs you as the employer two things: 1) the absent employee's pay for the day, and 2) the absent employee's *productivity* for the day.

So, as we think back to the previous chapter and all those expenses (especially relative to the small percentage of an operating budget that is your rent), would it surprise you to learn that having the kind of office people actually look forward to working in also cuts down on absenteeism? Give people a better place to work, and you'll be shocked by how much less often you get calls or emails about illness or a desire/need to work from home.

"So what?" you might think. "If Karen is out today, she'll just make up for lost time tomorrow." First, as far as assumptions go, it's a bit of a stretch to assume that Karen can do the work of two days in a single day. Second, if it's the office itself that is motivating Karen to take that sick day, how likely is she to be ultra-productive on her return?

There are bigger questions too. Who else in the company is impacted by Karen's absence? Does she have a staff that relies on her for input? Does she have a supervisor who needs her productivity to do his/her job correctly? And what are the total losses for any project that Karen or her team is contributing to?

In the US, it is estimated that the annual rate of absenteeism is 3%-4% per employee, based on the sector. This costs employers between $2,074 and $2,502 per employee per year.[5] We use the term "leakage" to describe the effect, because when one or two people are absent for a day or two in a week, it doesn't seem like a big deal, but it's kind of like a hole in a boat. It's a slow leak. It isn't noticeable at first, but over a

5 Various Authors. "Health, Wellbeing, and Productivity in Offices: The Next Chapter for Green Building." UKGBC. September 2017.

long period of time, you'll find yourself underwater. Assuming you fall somewhere into that national average, the way to calculate your own level of leakage is to first consider the number of employees you have, then multiply their average salaries by that 3-4% rate of absenteeism. What's your total leakage? Wouldn't it be nice if we could figure out ways to plug the hole, slow the leak, and make that number lower?

And brace yourself, because cost per employee is just the start of it. There are plenty of extremely complicated equations you can use to calculate exactly what absenteeism is costing you, but it all boils down to a whole lot of unpleasant multiples. Basically, you take Karen's weighted average hourly pay and flush that first. Then you add the cost of benefits per hour. Then you pile on the cost of lost hours of productivity for supervisors and staff. Then you multiply all that together before you even start considering what you're losing in terms of quality, delivery time of the work product, and the stress of any employees who have to pick up the slack for Karen.

Plus, we always have to keep in mind the customer effect. Every one of your customers who is used to working with Karen now either has to wait or accept working with someone he/she might not be familiar with. It's a little like trying to eat in a restaurant that's understaffed. One of the servers and one of the cooks called in sick this morning, and now your server is covering twice as many tables, and the cooks are overworked in the kitchen. But you, as the customer, aren't going to know this while you're waiting forever for your meal to arrive. All you're going to see is the slow service. That's going to impact your impression of this restaurant, and you might not come back again to change that opinion.

In short, never underestimate the staggering cost of absenteeism.

Having the kind of place that your people are proud of, a place where they enjoy being, and a place that makes them feel comfortable, happy, and healthy is a huge part of what gets them in the door every day. Let's say you're a little stressed out about a project you're working on, or about a supervisor who kind of came down on you yesterday. Or let's say your stress isn't even work-related. Maybe your son is having a tough time in school.

Whatever the source, you're just at your wits' end. You're having one of those melancholy mornings where you feel like getting ready and making that commute sounds like a more arduous undertaking than usual. If you work in a dull, depressing office, and you're thinking about that drab, enclosed workspace of yours, you're probably thinking sick day. But if you work in a dynamic space, where you're always comfortable, where the air is clean, where the lighting and art and paint colors are vibrant, and where so many of your friends will be waiting to greet you, then you're far, far more likely to suck it up and drive in to work. After all, if you called in sick, you wouldn't just be missing work; you'd be missing all that social interaction with your friends; you'd be missing your favorite lunch in the cafeteria; you'd be skipping out on your fitness time.

Exceptional office space (particularly for organizations that focus on health and wellness initiatives) can help improve employee cognition by 26% and reduce sick leave by as much as 30%.[6] Employees of these kinds of companies are far less likely to miss work, far more likely to be more productive while at work, and enjoy a better quality of life overall.

NO, SERIOUSLY. WHAT IS TURNOVER AND ABSENTEEISM REALLY COSTING YOU?

I'm afraid we're not done discussing costs yet. So far, we've only covered the ones we can see and measure. You can directly assess how painful it is to throw money at recruiting, orientation, interviewing, training, and reoutfitting new hires with their own fresh uniforms, computers, and equipment. You can measure how you might have to offer more money to each new hire you bring in, just to keep the flow going as your company in its increasingly outdated building becomes less and less competitive for talent.

In the case of turnover or chronic absenteeism, you might even be able to accept the new reality that you're going to have to rely on far less cost-efficient staffing strategies like hiring temps or offering overtime. Whatever the case, knowing the more tangible numbers at least prepares you for the prospect of shouldering the tremendous and largely

6 Gaskell, Adi. "A Green Office Equals a Productive Office." Forbes.com. February 15, 2017.

unnecessary expense of constantly having to replace your people or cover their absences.

But these are just the costs we can *see*. There's also a series of hidden costs associated with turnover and absenteeism—and they all come back to the cultural, morale, and engagement hits you're going to take thanks to that revolving door of new hires and exiting employees. Plus, don't forget the all-important customer issue I mentioned earlier.

If your company employs customer-facing staff who develop relationships with customers, then when that staff leaves, so does the relationship. Now you have to ask your customers to get acquainted with a whole new person, and this one probably isn't as knowledgeable or skilled as the departing employee simply because he/she hasn't had as much time in the job. If this happens often enough, you're eventually going to lose the customer too. In the meantime, you'll certainly lose sales in conjunction with that loss of knowledge about the product or service.

Out of all these hidden costs, though, we have to keep circling back to productivity. Think about the last time you tried something new. How about the last time you got a new smartphone? Now, if you're like me, you're always upgrading to the latest and greatest phone. I do this because I like the best technology, but the interesting part is that I upgrade even though I know it's going to cost me quite a bit of productivity in the short term. Even though the features of every new phone are mostly the same as those on the old one, I always spend the first week or so just trying to figure out how to *use* the thing.

It's the same effect with any new product or endeavor. It takes time to get used to new things, and time to master new skills. And if your new smartphone takes you a week to get a handle on, imagine how long it takes to adapt to and thrive in a new *job*. Every day that you have a new hire in a role formerly occupied by a talented employee is a day that is costing you considerable productivity and money.

Worse yet, that productivity loss extends to the other people on staff. Most people in a professional setting don't work alone. They count on other people's productivity to help drive their own. That new hire isn't just impacting his/her own work, but the work of everyone who works with him/her, as well. Plus, professional relationships have a tendency to elevate to the level of friendship.

If someone you count on, someone whose company you enjoy, someone you consider a *friend* suddenly leaves the company—if you go from being able to spend time together every day to maybe having to settle for just exchanging a message on social media once in a while—how is that going to make you feel? You're going to miss your friend. You're going to be stressed about not having that social outlet while also having to train this new guy to do what your friend used to do so well. Even if you don't mean for it to, your performance and quality of service is going to suffer, and so is the rest of the team's. This is exactly why turnover and absenteeism tend to negatively impact morale. It starts on the ground level and works its way up until it becomes a cancerous part of organizational culture.

When you factor in the unseen, indirect costs, some studies suggest that the expense for turnover is significantly higher than what we have already outlined. In fact, replacing a good employee might wind up costing you as much as *double* that employee's annual salary. Think about that for a moment. What's the average salary of your people? $30,000? $50,000? More? Double that number, and you've got a sense of how much turnover is costing you.[7]

Let's avoid making things too terrifying, though. Let's just focus on that original number that we calculated in the previous section—that $1.6 million annual fee for turnover. As Altman asks, what if we could reduce that rate by even just 20%? It's my position that moving into an inspiring new space with modern amenities will increase the rate of retention by *more* than 20%, but let's be conservative. At 20%, we're looking at a $320,000 per year savings on turnover alone.

The rent or construction costs of that new space might seem like a big expense now, but how does a *$3.2 million savings* over the next ten years sound? To me, it sounds slightly larger than the savings of $24,000 per year on rent (which, to be fair, calculates to a $240,000 savings over

7 Altman, Jack. "How Much Does Employee Turnover Really Cost?" Huffington Post. January 18, 2017.

the same ten-year period). $240,000 vs. $3.2 million. And that's just the savings for *turnover*—a savings that doesn't even factor in markedly lower rates of absenteeism, significantly lower operating expenses, and appreciably higher productivity levels across the board.

I find it kind of strange that most companies will spend tons of time and effort on strategies to minimize costs in every aspect of what they do... except for employee turnover and absenteeism. And that's especially strange because the largest operating expense line for almost every company is payroll. It's so logical, and yet so many business leaders ignore it: keeping your top employees improves productivity and profit (because seasoned employees are more efficient and effective employees); makes a staff more collaborative (because they've had more time to get to know each other); and leads to more innovation (because the longer you work on something and alongside the same knowledgeable people, the more opportunities you have to come up with disruptive solutions). Plus, cutting down on the cost of turnover allows you to reallocate those funds to more productive activities with higher ROI. And yet most companies don't pay any attention to the cost of high turnover or chronic absenteeism. Or worse, they just accept these factors as an inevitability.

Yes, the world has changed. And yes, the next ten years are going to bring higher and higher rates of turnover (at least for those companies that fail to adapt to this new environment). Millennials and Generation Z tend to job-hop more often than we ever did when we were in our twenties, and that trend will only continue. But none of this means that they're impossible to retain. That's the remarkable thing about people: it doesn't matter how young or old they are; if you give them what they want, they will be content, and if they're content, they'll show up for work more reliably, and over the long term, they'll *stay*.

In the end, if talented employees value office spaces with great amenities, and if losing talented employees is costing you anywhere from tens of thousands of dollars to double an average annual salary, then what exactly are you doing in an outdated office space?

CHAPTER 3

YOUR CULTURE ON *WOW*

"You never get a second chance to make a first impression."
- Will Rogers

What comes to mind when you picture the White House? For me, it's the incredible impression it makes. When you step into the White House, you say, "Wow!" And people have been saying that same thing for over 225 years. The White House is a big, impressive building decorated in a fashion that isn't just appealing, but also representative of US culture and the common purpose that the office of the president serves. What most people don't think about when they picture the White House is that it's also always on the cutting edge of technology and has lately begun to adapt to matters related to the health, wellness, and productivity of its staff.

Why do you think the White House is like that? Even from the day it was first designed by architect James Hoban in 1792, the reason was this: having a great space is like having home court advantage. Back when dignitaries still had to travel for weeks by boat to get to this country, being able to offer a setting where people actually *wanted* to meet gave the US and its leadership the upper hand. For one, they didn't have to be the people enduring that long boat passage. For another, if you put these visiting dignitaries up in a place as impressive as the White House, they're going to be more inclined to recognize your authority, and more knowledgeable about the culture and purpose you're serving.

The White House is, by its very nature, one of America's greatest examples of the power of the Wow Factor—which we define here as the many elements that combine to inspire, attract, and achieve the respect of the person stepping into the space for the first time. The Wow Factor is beauty, brilliance, style, distinction, vision, magnificence, vibe, and a little bit of luxury all rolled into one.

Photo: Careform – Architectural design by NEXT Architecture, photo by Mike Leonardi.

If you achieve the Wow Factor, and the immediate reaction of anyone entering your office space is to say, "Wow!" then your organization is better equipped to state your culture and purpose clearly, host meetings on your terms, close deals, recruit better people, retain more of your talent, and get higher productivity out of everyone you count on.

Plus, let's not underestimate how much value there is in having people come to you. Sure, we're not talking about months-long boat passages anymore, but if your office is so great that people actually *prefer* to have their meetings there, then you're no longer losing time to the commute to someone else's office or meeting space, you don't have to search and pay for parking, and when the meetings are over, everyone who works for you is just steps away from the space where they can be most productive.

That's the power of the home court advantage. And of course, these are just the ancillary benefits. If you work in a place that makes people say "Wow!" when they walk in the door, then you're also enjoying a huge advantage in the talent war. On top of that, just like Lynne Schultz at Waldron Private Wealth, every person who works for you takes great pride in the physical location where they work. That pride goes a long way not just toward culture, but toward the kind of effort you can expect out of your people. If you love the place you work, you take greater ownership in your role and your employer's success. You also buy in more readily to the company's culture. Home court advantage, better recruiting, greater buy-in from your staff—this is the power of enhancing your culture with the Wow Factor.

So now that we've taken a deep dive into the terrifying amounts that an outdated space can cost you in turnover and absenteeism, let's flip the script and look at *why* and *how* a space with the Wow Factor can rev the RPMs of your business by helping you win the talent war, heighten employee productivity, and both make you *and* save you more money.

THE LUXURY HOTEL VIBE

As we covered in the previous chapter, employee turnover costs money. Lots of it. So, the natural next question is how do we minimize that turnover? And the answer starts with another question: What do you think is the main reason employees leave for other employers? Better salary? Better benefits? Better job security? No, no, and no. For the past decade, the trend has increasingly leaned toward opportunities for career growth, a desire to escape a lousy boss, a desire to find a better social fit with coworkers, and finally, cultural factors. And if we're talking strictly about the two younger generations in the workforce, 84% of them rank "a sense of purpose" as the top reason to either stay with or leave an employer.[1]

Put another way, more and more people are leaving organizations for professional, social, and lifestyle factors rather than financial. In huge numbers, today's workers want to feel like they are a part of something meaningful. They want to contribute to a company that is committed to bettering their lives and the lives of others. They want to work in teams with people who actually enjoy spending time together. They want a leader who makes it clear that he or she cares about their wellbeing. They want to be part of a positive, fulfilling culture.

There was a time when the answer to meeting these demands included better leadership training and a strong human resources department. Great leadership and HR are still incredibly important, of course, but these days, the physical makeup of the office plays a huge role, as well. This is because there is no other factor in a professional setting that sends a clearer message about how much leadership cares about its people. In this way, having a strong, engaging office space is better than changing your leadership communication strategies or strengthening the HR approach. It's the difference between leading by speaking and leading by example. The former strategies are about talking the talk. Giving your staff a space they truly love to be in is *walking the walk*.

You want to compel more of your people to stay? Then use your office space as a supplemental tool and as a means to communicate that this is a place where career growth is possible. Show them how much leadership cares by providing them the kind of comfort and luxury they can't even get at home. Help them meet their social needs through engaging collaborative and social space. Connect your physical environment with the culture of your business, and they'll start to see that all-important sense of purpose too.

---

1 Sellers, Patricia. "Millennials Want This One Thing from Employers." Fortune.com. July 15, 2015.

When you think about it, it seems so simple: if they're more comfortable and have more of their needs met at work than at home, it makes it that much harder to decide to leave for another employer. It's a little like the vacation factor. The last time you went on vacation and checked in to a luxury hotel or resort, chances are pretty good that you felt a sense of longing to stay beyond that week or two you originally scheduled (if only for a while longer). Yes, part of that is because vacation absolves you from the more stressful responsibilities of your work and home life, but don't underestimate the pull of luxurious amenities, easy access to food, drink, fitness, spa, and services, and the incredible benefit that is the concierge desk.

The same is true about retention. If one of my employees is thinking about leaving the company, they're going to have to think long and hard about leaving behind the café and fitness center, the half-day Fridays, the flexible work schedule, and the extra services we provide them to help them meet their daily needs. One more compelling reason to stay is that, in their search for another employer, they're going to want to narrow their prospects to other companies that provide these same amenities and services—and how many companies out there are doing these things? Not that many.

And another good reason: the more you can make your office feel like a luxury hotel, the more work feels a little like a luxury vacation. But unlike vacation, all these luxuries don't make people take it easy. Quite the contrary. Amenities and services that drop stress levels at work lead to huge improvements in productivity and also a stronger desire for the average employee to stay.

The goal as we head toward the peak of the talent war shouldn't be just about improving leadership skills and softening our cultural practices. There is a humanization of the corporation occurring in this country. More and more companies are recognizing that you keep people by showing them you care about them. Part of that is understanding the work-life blend—understanding that if you leave in the middle of the day for a program at your kid's school, or if you take an hour to use the fitness center after lunch, that's fine because there's a give and take about when you get your work done. The next logical step in this humanization transformation is to find ways to make our physical spaces feel more like they are driven by *hospitality* than just plain *work*.

If you want to retain more of your people, then giving them reason to view the office as their second home is step one. Getting them to view it as a place that is more comfortable and enjoyable to be in than their *own* home is step two. Then, the final step is creating a space and offering services that are so luxurious that they start sharing it on social media. When they're Instagramming the awesomeness of their sit-stand desk, the perfect foam on the coffee from the café, or scenes from the food truck, yoga class, or mobile car wash service in the parking lot, then you know you have an uncommon level of their loyalty. You know you're that much more likely to compel them to stay beyond the typical shelf-life of employees from younger generations (which is a startling *three years or less* for organizations that don't offer these amenities and services[2]).

The truth is that this isn't about younger vs. older employees either. *Everyone* likes the amenities and the concierge desk at the luxury resort, and they like it for the same reasons: convenience is nice. Comfort is nice. Having the ability to choose from any number of engaging settings to spend our time is nice. We *all* seek these things, no matter how old we are.

Plus, don't underestimate how profoundly these measures can impact the lives of a more aged workforce. Boomers might be heading toward retirement, but that doesn't mean they're immune to the desire to leave for another employer. And the obvious part about talent is that it tends to grow with age. Keeping your younger employees around longer should be a goal, but your most talented and seasoned veterans are likely to come from the Generation X and Boomer groups. If we're talking about the financial damage of turnover, there's nothing quite like watching thirty years of experience walk out the door.

In fact, the irreplaceable experience and difficult-to-replace skills that exist in the Boomer and Gen X generations is a significant contributor to the growing talent war. As tens of millions of talented people from

---

2 Meister, Jeanne. "The Future of Work: Job Hopping Is the 'New Normal' for Millennials." Forbes.com. August 14, 2012.

both these generations gear up for retirement, and as many millions more consider mid-to-late-career changes, employers are scrambling to figure out how to fill the skills and knowledge gaps. This is a particular challenge, given that the Boomer generation is considerably larger than Gens X, Y, and Z. In many industries, there just aren't enough talented people available to replace the exiting workforce.

As with younger generations, the best strategy here is to find ways to keep Boomers comfortable, happy, and feeling like your organization helps them meet their needs in a genuinely unique (and equally irreplaceable) way. This helps keep them under your employ for longer, helps you fill a higher percentage of the soon-to-be-vacant roles with highly talented people, and helps departing employees train younger people to absorb more of their talent. In this way, a well-designed office with a luxury hotel vibe isn't just a lure for new people, or a compulsion for existing employees to stay; it is also a more comfortable and productive environment for training and retraining to help your organization bridge the talent gap.

YOUR LEADERSHIP + YOUR SPACE = YOUR CULTURE

In concert with the humanization of the corporation, typical organizational structure has changed pretty drastically over the past decade or so. Most forward-thinking companies don't align themselves into hierarchies anymore. It's a flatter, more networked structure of employee interaction, leadership, and roles.

The world's best companies aren't treating their people like their subordinates; rather, they're *empowering* their people to take greater responsibility, own their positions, self-evaluate their annual performances, better themselves, innovate, and contribute to the greater good of the enterprise. They've gone from lock-and-key office space to a greater sense of transparency in everything they do. Where before, the message was "work hard so we can profit," the message has become, "let's work well together to serve our company's purpose, and the money will follow."

And while the growing wave of younger generations in the workforce has contributed to much of the shift in thinking, it would be a mistake to assume that they are alone in wanting these changes. It doesn't matter who you are, where you come from, or what your age; there's a pretty strong chance you value a sense of belonging to something bigger than yourself, and more importantly, a chance to contribute and feel like you've made a difference.

All those cultural changes I mentioned in the previous paragraph speak to those universal desires. Help your people feel like those desires are being met, and they will work better, smarter, and harder for your company, they'll call in sick less frequently, and they'll stay under your employ for longer. Show prospective employees that you offer them the best chance to have those needs met, and you'll win those talented recruits more often.

So, how do we get there? As the equation that serves as the title to this section suggests, the way your culture is shaped and perceived starts with your leadership. You have to be the one sincerely leading this change. Put simply, if you care, they care. You have to find ways to make everyone feel welcome and a part of the "family" that is your organization. Through your leadership, you can provide that sense of belonging, those opportunities to make contributions, and that feeling that every employee's role truly makes a difference (for your company, for its mission, and ideally, for the world).

The second component of the equation is of course your space. This is because your space is so much more than just the place where your people work (and where your recruits may or may not hope to work); it's a complement to your culture. Ideally, your space should be designed in a way that reflects the culture you're trying to promote. It should be a physical demonstration of what motivates your people and your recruits to care about the company and work hard at what they do. Back in the early 2000s, when everyone else was trying to figure out whether this whole Internet thing had a future in the professional world, Joe Blattner, founder of a dynamic Pittsburgh marketing firm today known as Brunner Inc., was busy changing the way we think about how office space can reflect a company's culture and purpose.

A little background on Blattner: in addition to founding Brunner (which, before he sold his ownership stake, was known as Blattner Brunner, Inc., an integrated marketing services firm synonymous with quality and exceptional creativity), he now serves as a strategy consultant and owner of two software-as-a-service business enterprises. Blattner Brunner was a startup in Pittsburgh long before startups in Pittsburgh were so widespread. From their beginnings in the early 90s, they steadily grew into the kind of name recognition that, by the aughts, saw them dubbed one of the top ten brands of the decade. Of course they owe a great deal of this to their cultural and managerial style—to say nothing of the high quality of their work product—but if you ask Blattner, an awful lot of their success had to do with the spaces they occupied.

Long before they took on the Blattner Brunner name, the company set up shop in the kinds of offices that were all too typical in the 70s and 80s. The executives made their spaces in closed-door rooms with the staff out in the open—first in open desks, and later in cubicles. "It was bland, cheap space," Blattner said. "It didn't fit what we were trying to do as a company."

What concerned them most back then was distributed processing. Most companies at the time were heavy into figuring out how to integrate computers as tools into their increasingly networked workflows, but by the end of the 90s, Blattner and Brunner (or the "Killer Bs," as they were known) were pivoting toward figuring out how to make their staff more collaborative, creative, and willing to learn together in the physical space of their office. "If you're looking for creative collaboration like we were," Blattner said, "then open office just makes sense. It helped us demonstrate to our clients and prospects how an integrated marketing team could work together across many different platforms."

Given their goals, the idea of enclosed offices seemed antithesis to what a creative company should be doing. The concept of sticking executives and other key personnel into boxed spaces with closed doors meant removing your top minds not only from the collaborative process, but from daily opportunities to teach and mentor the rest of the staff, as well. Closed doors prevent seasoned veterans and highly talented managers from taking a newer employee under their wing and helping him or her grow and learn. This can be problematic for any company looking to grow its capabilities, but it's especially damaging for startups and small companies with lower budgets for official training programs. "A closed office provides your most expensive people the opportunity to separate themselves from the day to day business of the company," Blattner said. "Being able to close a door allows a person to get more involved in their personal business and less in your business. It promotes secrets instead of collaboration. Call it paranoia, but to me, closed offices just didn't serve the interest of what our company considered the greater good. Giving people places to hide can only hurt a collaborative organization."

Of course it would be folly to think that we can expect our people to leave their personal lives at home, especially in this era of the work-life blend. And there are obviously times when a manager needs to share something with a staff member that is better to remain private. This is why, despite advocating against enclosed offices, every time Blattner Brunner upgraded their offices over the years, their designs retained sufficient designated space that allowed for privacy. These spaces simply weren't dedicated offices. Where privacy was necessary, employees could visit a conference room or other collaborative space, where a door could be closed for the duration of the need.

As the company grew over the years, it enjoyed a trio of key moves, each one more successful than the last. First, in 1994, they grew into the lease of a single floor in a Class A space. 1998 saw a second move into a space that allowed them to correct a few of the mistakes in their first design (mistakes they learned about the hard way). Then, with their firm expanding rapidly, they made a huge splash in their industry with a move over their lifetime from C-rated buildings to A-rated buildings, all in downtown Pittsburgh. One of these moves coincided with a dramatic redesign of a space in a high-quality building formerly occupied by Westinghouse.

Along the way, there was some trial and error. Some things worked and others didn't. But what remained was the central philosophy: our space must reflect our culture. The more the space invited collaboration, the more collaboration actually happened. Through each move, the company benefitted from its staff having access to leadership, opportunities for collaboration and learning, and the dramatic improvement in productivity that comes naturally from people being able to interact and *see* each other working.

So as we move forward with our discussion of why and how dynamic office space can impact your RPMs, keep in mind that culture and leadership have to lead this change. Yes, temperature, air quality, lighting, and quality of materials matters a great deal, but so does the message you're sending with your layout and décor. That open work flow with multiple and varied places for people to get their work in somewhere other than at their desk ensures that everyone has a chance to bump into each other and share ideas, while also allowing them to find a quiet place to work without distraction when the time calls for it. Further, every little personal touch you put into the building materials, the art, the music, the aromas in the air (like enticing food and coffee), and the technology all around the office helps shape your culture.

The message here is simple: don't just design the floor plan without consulting and considering what your people prefer. Don't slap some expensive art on the wall, toss some beanbag chairs in a lounge, and call it a day. Be mindful of the cultural message you're trying to send. Involve your people in the design. Solicit their feedback on what will or won't work for them. Then, invest in a layout that is reflective of the kind of working environment you're collectively hoping to promote. Make your art reflect your company's purpose. Celebrate your people with photos on the walls, announcements of their accomplishments, and depictions of contributions, just like you celebrate your family at home. These might sound like complicated or even expensive steps, but the reward is in some ways beyond measure.

THEY APPRECIATE LUXURY AMENITIES, EVEN IF THEY DON'T USE THEM

Even the people who aren't all in on these amenities and this lifestyle stuff still do care about it. Not everyone will use the café or the collaborative spaces or the fitness center. Not everyone will flow around the office, talking to people from multiple different roles and setting up shop to work in several different spots over the course of a day. But this is just because not everyone is wired to work that way. Even for these people, and even for this kind of recruit, the power of having these amenities is every bit as formidable. Just knowing that they have the option to use these amenities still goes a long way.

Consider this: At the Bentley, even the people who don't use our fitness center pictured below are still proud to tell their friends and family that we have one. And our beautiful café and conference rooms have contributed to our recruiting and retention efforts on more than one occasion with people who won't even be working directly in our office. Even those employees who wind up working in the field are still proud of our home office. As a source of pride, the Bentley has worked its way into the fabric of our culture. You really can't put a price tag on that.

Further, the Bentley has reshaped who we are as a company by positioning us better for the future. Our culture is stronger, our people are closer, absenteeism is down, and everyone isn't just happy about their jobs, but *excited* to come into work each day. On the recruiting front, we've hired some extremely talented people in the past year—people who probably wouldn't have considered us, had we been in our previous office. But now, just like the White House, we can present an environment that makes it clear how we're always leaning forward, on the cutting edge, and poised to impress (and grow).

Just as importantly, our space is the perfect representation of how much leadership cares about the people who work here. We have spent a great deal of time, effort, and money on helping our strong culture come together, but our office space is an essential piece of the equation. It demonstrates that we want everyone to be comfortable, healthy, and happy at work. That message resonates from top to bottom, and from inside to outside the organization. And as everyone knows, happy employees make for happy customers.

USE YOUR SPACE WELL

I often hear two counterpoints to the above. The first one goes like this: "We have an old, outdated office and our culture is fine." The second is the opposite: "I already have a great, modern space, but we don't have any of these cultural benefits you're talking about." These are the two primary reasons that there are *two* components to the cultural equation we discussed earlier. It's possible to have bad space and great culture, and it's possible to have great space and bad culture. It all comes down to how you, as a leader, promote the *use* of that space. In other words, it's not enough to just move into better space. How you use your space matters. While the building sets the tone and serves as a subliminal message for how much leadership cares about its people, the action leadership takes to build a culture around that space matters just as much.

Recently, I toured an excellent building. It had all the bells and whistles. The technology was flashy, there was plenty of collaborative space, lots of natural light, and both the lobby and the café were impressive. But when I arrived for the tour, the representative who was showing me around had to ask me to wait for a moment so she could lock her office door. All this potential collaborative space, and every office was enclosed, every door locked. As we toured, I quickly realized that all the conference rooms were empty, no one used the café, and almost no one spoke to each other, let alone felt a kinship with each other and the business. The people who worked in this beautiful office weren't part of a culture that promoted a collective contribution to a greater good. They were all about locking their own spaces and guarding their own information.

Now, you might be reading this and thinking, "What's wrong with that?" Presently, there are plenty of companies that operate in this way, and some of them even achieve growth and sustained success. But in the years to come, thanks to all these demographic trends we've been discussing, that is going to change. The amenities in offices like these are nice, but without a cultural promotion of collaboration, sharing of information, and comradery among staff, they will lack the innovation, free-flowing of information, collaborative productivity, and Wow Factor that attracts and retains the most talented people.

So, again, let's be mindful of the message we're sending as leaders. We want to meet this cultural change, embrace it, and show our staffs that we care. If you're going to use your space in the best possible way, it helps to know what your people want in their space. Today, a large percentage of people want mobility and freedom. This is the society that the Internet has brought upon us. Look at the global stage. Information flows instantly. The walls are down. Whether you work in America, Europe, Russia, China, India—it doesn't matter—you can share your work product freely. There are no walls separating (most) countries from one another. The same needs to be true at work.

To drive this culture, it's important to remember that ease of use is priority #1. Accessibility to work—whether on site or remotely—is a huge factor. Flexible hours might sound like a fad, but it's the new normal, and will remain that way. Today, it's easier to live than ever before. It's easier to buy things. Easier to acquire the services you need. Everything is more convenient. And it's only going to get more so in the years to come.

If we're going to win that near-term talent war, then we have to find ways to embrace these trends and reflect them not just in our office space, but in our cultures. So let's take a look at how to create an office space with the Wow Factor, and more importantly, how to *use* that space well for strengthening our culture and improving our recruiting.

NEVER UNDERESTIMATE THE REFRESHING POWER OF *MOVING AROUND*

It might surprise you to learn that most people would prefer *not* to spend all day in their assigned workspaces. A high percentage of people across all generations enjoy the option to be able to move around a little and complete their productive work in multiple spaces over the course of the day.[3] If there are comfortable conference rooms, quiet spaces, lounge areas, sit-stand desks, ball seating, or walking treadmills, they will move around between these spaces more often than not.

And this is true no matter how awesome you make their personal workspaces. Millennials and Generation Z are particularly fond of this office mobility, agility, and variability, but they certainly aren't the only ones who favor having options. People just like being able to change their environments. When you're at home, you probably don't spend all your time in one room of the house. The same is true at work (or at least it should be).

The more you're forced to sit at the same desk and stare at the same screen and the same décor and the same enclosed space, the less productive you're going to be. Conversely, if you're able to seek out a space that suits your preferences for comfort, quiet (or unquiet), lighting, and vibe, then you start your work with a fresher mind and a sense that all your needs have been met. Think about it: when you're doing your work at home, where do you go? Probably the first place you go is where you're most comfortable. But just as probably, that's not the *only* space you occupy while you're completing that work. You move around. You change things up. You find ways to keep your mind actively engaged by varying the space in which you're working.

This effect doesn't just help different employees meet different personal preferences and needs; it reduces eyestrain (from having to stare at the same screen against the same backdrop all day), relieves muscle tension in the neck, shoulders, and back (from sitting in the same position in the same chair all day), and lowers work-related stress (by allowing for more collaboration, comradery, and a chance to unwind in a more productive way).

As we'll see in a later chapter, all these factors drastically improve productivity. Consider, also, that while open floor plans can improve collaboration and innovation, not everyone does their best work in an open setting. Some people just prefer quiet while they're grinding out their work. For these people—and for anyone, really—every distraction,

3 Hoskins, Diane. "Employees Perform Better When They Can Control Their Space." Harvard Business Review. January 16, 2014.

however minor, can lead to up to twenty minutes of lost productivity. Each time you're jarred out of the zone, after all, it takes a while to get back into it.

Further, think about one of those days when your computer was just really, really slow. I know that sort of thing seems to happen every time I'm in a long line at the airport ticketing desk. "The system is just so slow today," is the inevitable reason for the delay. That same concept applies to every piece of technology on which your company relies. It isn't just faster computers that will reduce distraction and improve productivity, but so will faster WiFi, more touchscreen interaction, and more seamless connectivity between personal monitors and the monitors in your meeting and social spaces.

Better technology also helps send the message that leadership is willing to invest in the staff's comfort and make their jobs easier to do. At Burns Scalo, we lease our technology so that we can ensure that everything is replaced and updated every two to three years. Why wait for these important tools to break or slow down before you replace them—especially considering how an upgrade in technology generates *immediate* payback in the form of improved productivity?

Plus, regular upgrades can enhance your culture tremendously. By using technology upgrades to show our employees that we care about their comfort and ability to do their jobs, they show us greater loyalty and productivity in return. A slightly more expensive investment in technology leads to a significant return in our employees taking ownership of their work, and in the company as a whole.

And all of this absolutely nails it on the recruiting front. Once again, it all comes down to choice. If you're a talented recruit, and you walk into an office where you can sense that you're going to have one place to work (your desk), very few opportunities to change scenery and seek comfort, and you'll be using outdated technology, you're probably thinking about only one thing in that interview room: the rigors of the job you're being asked to do.

If you interview in an office with the Wow Factor—if you can see yourself doing some of your work at your workspace on a top-of-the-line laptop plugged in to multiple monitor screens, some in the lounge, and some in a flashy conference room where you can instantly click-share your screen to the monitor or projector, then you're not just thinking about the job itself; you're thinking about the lifestyle you'll get to enjoy. And if the person interviewing you is demonstrating that sincerity that he/she cares about his/her employees, then you're also thinking about cultural fit. When your recruits start having more of these thoughts, the tide of the talent war starts turning in your favor.

HOW TO ACHIEVE THE WOW FACTOR

We know two things for certain: 1) the growing talent war means that the best people have more choices about where to work than ever before; and 2) due to a combination of cultural and technological factors, people now have more choices about where they *perform* their work. If we're going to win the talent war, and also get people into the office, where they can be more productive, then the first and best step is to upgrade your office to the Wow Factor. We need to find ways to use your physical space as a means to leave a lasting, meaningful impression. To get there, we must remember that there is always a market for quality, and luxury has no limits on price.

Achieving the Wow Factor begins with putting yourself in the shoes of someone seeing your office space for the first time. Then, as you pursue design or seek upgrades, the effort extends to getting input from your people on what makes them comfortable, and what they value in a workplace. If you go to the expense to make your people feel as if you are meeting their needs in a more luxurious way, your culture will greatly benefit, which will in turn improve your recruiting and retention, and for that matter, drive the full picture of your company's RPMs.

Whichever choices you make on redefining your space, there are five main components to the Wow Factor. They are:

1. LIGHT QUALITY

Here is one of the most logical statements I can make: people are physically equipped to work best in natural light. In the absence of genuine daylight, sources designed to mimic natural light work well. Further, the level and intensity of light matters a great deal. Appropriate light quality and level can reduce eye strain, manage stress, and elevate mood—all of which contribute to heightened productivity.

The Riviera: Architectural design by NEXT Architecture.

Many companies have gone to LED lighting, as it tends to contribute to the wellness factors listed above. But it's also less costly. The bulbs have longer life, which saves on the cost and human resources required to replace them. I know with our management group, the top task every day is to change light bulbs, so installing LEDs can cut down on that work. Plus, they don't consume as much electricity, and they burn cooler, which means they don't contribute ambient heat, thereby making it less costly to cool the space to the appropriate temperature.

The technology on this front gets better every year, as well. Lately, some companies have started implementing what is called "daylight harvesting," which is a light management technique that changes the level of overhead lighting based on the corresponding level of ambient light present in the space. Put simply, when the natural light from outside is stronger, the overhead lighting dims. When there's less light streaming in from outside, the overhead lights get brighter. We enjoy this feature at the Bentley, because not only does it help meet all those eye-strain, stress, and mood-related needs, but it saves significantly on the electricity bill. Most don't notice it's even happening on anything more than a subconscious level, but if you're subconsciously more comfortable, then you're also less often distracted and more often productive.

On the recruiting front, the quality of light changes so much about a person's impression of a space, whether it's consciously or subconsciously noticed. If you have better lighting, it goes a long way toward the Wow Factor, which directly leads to hiring those great recruits more frequently.

2. AIR QUALITY

Just like sub-optimal lighting can be a drag on job performance, there's nothing quite like stale or otherwise unpleasant air to distract someone from his/her work. And the temperature of the surrounding environment can be one of the most considerable unseen contributors to productivity levels. I'm sure this is the same at every office, but the number one service call for our management company is complaints about the temperature being too hot or too cold.

There are many reasons for this—some people sit in the center of the office, where it's warmer compared to spaces near the glass; rapid fluctuation of outdoor temperatures can quickly impact the temperature inside; and in most business settings, men tend to wear pants, which are on the warmer side, while women sometimes wear dresses or skirts, which are obviously less primed for the cold—but the message is simple: it's tough to focus when the temperature is uncomfortable. Newer buildings typically offer systems that allow for more flexibility from room to room in a space, but there are controls you can install in any building, no matter its age or the quality of its HVAC, that will make the temperatures more uniform and comfortable throughout the building.

The humidity level of the air also contributes not just to your productivity, but your overall wellbeing. We'll talk a little more about this effect in the next chapter, but for now, keep in mind that the air you breathe contributes far more to your wellness, and to your perception of the company's culture, than you realize. Better air means more comfort, and a more comfortable employee means better performance.

Autodesk: Architectural design by NEXT Architecture, photo by Mike Leonardi

3. MUSIC

People often turn up their nose at the idea that music can contribute to the impression of an office, most likely because too many people think of music as a social element, and not a professional one. But there are reasons that strictly social spaces so often feature music. It sets the vibe. It taps into the listener's emotions. It contributes to bonding between groups of people. Why *wouldn't* you want that same sort of power in your office space? Especially since it makes such a good impression not just on your people, but on the people who visit your office. I can't tell you how many of our clients have complimented us on the music we play throughout our building.

The best businesses play music in the lobby at the very least. Others put it in the restrooms, the café, the fitness center, the outdoor space, and the elevator. The music is always pleasant and engaging. It isn't Muzak-style tunes, either, but actual songs that resonate with a broad and varied audience. And it's never stale, as it rotates regularly.

In December, it's holiday music. For the country fans, it'll be country one week, and for the independent music fans, it's indie rock the next. At Burns Scalo, we let our employees choose the music on a rotating basis. Some of us like oldies. Others like 90s-era pop. No matter what the genre, the goal is to feature a mix, and to allow everyone the chance to feel like they're contributing, you value their opinions, and they are included with the group. On top of that, just having music in these social spaces sets the vibe, gets people talking and interacting, and improves the overall mood (and productivity) of the staff.

4. FOOD

Food is such an overlooked element. For many of the leaders who refuse to accept food as the kind of amenity they need to provide for their staff, it all comes back to that idea of, "It's just a free banana. Get to work!" But I'm here to tell you, it's so much more than a free banana. Or almonds. Or gourmet coffee. The food you provide does two key things, and it does them extremely well. First, it shows the employees that you care about their needs. It sends the message that you want them to be healthy, well-fueled, and never hungry. Second, it subtly encourages people to eat better, and people who eat better work harder, smarter, and more effectively.[4]

4 Friedman, Ron. "What You Eat Affects Your Productivity." Harvard Business Review. October 17, 2014.

Another rather underappreciated factor is that if you offer healthy foods in the café, employees no longer need to spend the time it takes to go fiddle with the vending machine for that candy bar or those chips that are just going to cause them to sugar-crash an hour later. They're less likely to be compelled to leave the office to pick up some fast food. When the choice is to spend an hour driving to McDonald's so you can spend the afternoon feeling lousy or go to the café to grab an apple and granola bar, you'd be amazed at how most people (at least eventually) prefer the latter. This goes back to the convenience part of the equation we discussed earlier. More and more people are looking to have multiple needs met by their workplace. Health, wellness, and good food—these are the most no-brainer ways to do exactly that.

It's not just a free banana. It's a subtle (but significant) way to give the people what they want. Meanwhile, you're leading them toward healthier behavior. You don't need to provide full meals, but healthy snacks can make a massive difference. In our office, the food was something people appreciated at first, but now it's something they *count on* as part of their daily routine. It's part of what hooks them about coming in to work. We buy bananas by the crate. They're delivered on Mondays, and they're gone by Wednesday.

Where before, people would go to the nearby Starbucks to pick up a sugary drink and a pastry, now they're in our café making smoothies, grabbing snacks, and soon, they'll be drinking from our barista-style gourmet coffee maker. And while they're doing this, they're all *talking to each other.* People who don't even work directly with each other exchange ideas on their work, which leads to bigger and better and more collaborative ideas. This incredibly simple investment has led to healthier, more productive, more connected people, and it has made our culture ever more cohesive.

By the way, one final thought about food: it's not enough just to pick three or four healthy foods and set them out. Sure, people care about this stuff, but people also get tired of eating the same thing over and over again. Everything runs its course. You've got to keep that campfire burning by putting new logs on it once in a while. Don't keep buying the same granola bar for years and years without change. Sub out the almonds for some pistachios every once in a while. In the fall, get some maple flavors and pumpkin spice in the place. Around the holidays, serve traditional holiday foods. And most importantly, seek input from your staff. Ask your people what healthy snacks they enjoy, and then put those foods on a quarterly or seasonal rotation.

5. TECHNOLOGY

Here's something every business leader needs to accept: it doesn't matter what our company does; we're *all* in the technology business. At Burns Scalo, we think we're in the commercial real estate business, but watch what happens when a key system slows down or a computer breaks for a day. The productivity of anyone who relies on that system or computer grinds to a halt. And heaven forbid our WiFi ever goes down. Might as well send everybody home at that point.

Technology is so much more than just the tools your people use to do their jobs. It is the lifeblood of the whole company. If you're not regularly investing in new and better technology, you're going to pay for it in different ways. And believe me, you can't afford to wait until it breaks.

Think about your office technology like you think about your car. You can't just drive it and drive it and drive it and expect it to run forever. Eventually you have to change the oil or put new tires on it. And later, no matter what you do, it's going to break down at some point. It's for these two reasons that I prefer to lease my car. Every three years, I get a new one. I'm always still happy with my car by the end of the term, but I get the new one anyway because a dealer once told me that the technology in these things doubles every eighteen months. So, even though it isn't something I need, I go in for it anyway. People respond to the chance at having the latest and greatest technology. It inspires me to upgrade my car, and it will inspire your staff to work harder with the flashy new tools they have been given.

It's not just the computers and WiFi either. Yes, the flat screen TVs are impressive. Recruits and employees alike do tend to enjoy being able to easily "click-share" their laptop screens with a presentation screen in any room. As a bonus, that kind of thing drives collaboration and productivity. At the Bentley, one of our best conversation pieces is the snap-glass that surrounds our main conference room—flick a light switch, and the transparent glass walls instantly become opaque, turning the room from open to private. There are hundreds of touches like these that can improve the way your company is perceived from a technological perspective, but what really matters most is how you use that technology to promote your culture.

The solar panels on the roof send the message that your company cares about the environment. Better light, air, and temperature control technology sends the message that you care about your staff's health and wellbeing. But the most powerful and often overlooked role that technology can play is the one I mentioned earlier in the chapter: people appreciate upgrades. There's nothing quite like telling someone they're getting a new computer, and then having them say, "What do you mean I'm getting a new computer? There's nothing wrong with mine." The message then becomes, "That's exactly right. But I don't want to wait until something goes wrong, or it slows down. I want you to always be comfortable with your computer, and to always know that you have the newest, best, and fastest technology."

There's just something about our modern relationship with technology. Announce that you're giving everyone an extra holiday, and they'll appreciate it. Announce that you're giving them all a new cell phone or computer, or a second monitor, or faster WiFi, and you'll be hearing the buzz for weeks. Every time they look at their phone, they'll be reminded about how much you care. In a truly remarkable way, technology has become completely interwoven with our culture outside the workplace. The more you can use it to enhance the culture of your business, the stronger the message becomes that you care about your people and your productivity soars.

DELTA POINT:
DO RIGHT BY THEM; THEY'LL DO RIGHT BY YOU

Yes, the Wow Factor helps us recruit better people and keep the best ones. It is still all about people and money. But you know what? Along the way, it feels good to do right by people too. It's incredibly rewarding to help people achieve their dreams, to give them autonomy and empowerment, and to watch them lead a higher quality of work-life blend and grow as a result. And it's really rewarding to create an environment full of brotherhood and sisterhood, where people genuinely care about each other and feel like they belong to the place as something more than just employees. Using your physical space as a means to enhance your brand and culture is a little like creating a fraternity or sorority. The space becomes so much more than a workplace. It becomes part of the group's identity.

By making this investment in your office space, by increasing the delta of your rent by a remarkably small percentage, and by investing in the wellbeing of your people, you're helping them to make the world a better place, contribute to society, and enhance your own calling as a leader. As a benefit, profits tend to follow these positive vibes. That's the lasting power of the Wow Factor. It revs the RPMs. It enhances your space, improves your culture, allows your people to lead healthy, happy, and productive personal and professional lives, paves the way for future leaders of your company, and strengthens your legacy—all while it makes your company more profitable.

CHAPTER 4

IF YOU RENT IT, THEY WILL COME

"There are three things that matter in property:
Location, location, location."
- Lord Harold Samuel

We've all heard that old Lord Samuel song a million times, but today, it has taken on a brand-new meaning. Back when Lord Samuel was coining that nugget, it used to be that the best locations were simply the ones you could *see*. Yes, visibility is still a nice benefit if you can get it, but where you choose to set up shop also speaks (and louder than ever before) to what you stand for as a company and exactly *who* you're trying to recruit to work for you.

So, as we engage with a talent war that is only going to intensify over the decade to come, we have to embrace the notion that location matters in so many ways beyond visibility. Finding the right location is important no matter what size your company, small, medium, or large. The goal is to position your business in a location that will help you attract the most and best talent. To paraphrase the classic movie *Field of Dreams*, "If you [rent] it, they will come."

Let's start with the large category. When I first spoke to the leaders of the rapidly growing energy company Rice Energy, I learned quickly that they had been through the wringer on just about every location issue a company can face. They had six offices scattered all over the suburbs and had seen just how much of a productivity-suck that kind of thing can be. This sparked a decision to choose a single office large enough where they could move all of their staff.

"We outgrew the central office before we even moved into it," said Jamie Rogers, a senior vice president with the company prior to its recent sale. "At that point, it seemed pretty clear that we would have to build our own space that we would have room to grow into. But we'd just invested all this energy in trying to get into a central office, so the idea of building

---

Photo: Arcadia Healthcare Solutions – Architectural design by NEXT Architecture, photo by Mike Leonardi.

the next headquarters didn't seem like it would be supported by the executive level and the board."

But when Jamie proposed the concept to his CEO, the immediate response was, "I don't know how we have a choice at this point."

So Rice Energy, having just coordinated a big move, would now begin planning another one. There would be all the work to do on choosing representatives and architects and builders, of course, and even more work to do on designing a space that reflected their culture.

"We didn't just want a bigger space," Jamie explained. "We wanted to make sure that whatever we designed and built would reflect our identity as a company." But before all that work could begin, Rice Energy had to determine the best location—one that would be easily accessible in terms of transportation; one that would allow their employees to have as many of their personal and professional needs met as efficiently as possible; one that would offer the kind of visibility that could put their grand design on display and help raise their brand; and one that would fit the message of who they were and what they stood for as a company.

Getting all this right would require some investment in time, and a great deal of study, but as John Waldron soon discovered after beginning his own search for a new location for Waldron Private Wealth, the investment in time and study is essential. "The deeper we got into this, the more we realized we *had* to get into it," John said. "When we started looking for a new location, that was the ah-ha moment for us. We saw that this was our best opportunity to create something that would announce who we are as a company. So we said, 'Let's get it right, make the right investment, and really take advantage of this unique opportunity we have.'"

Now, both these companies moved into newly developed buildings, but you don't have to build just to meet your specific location needs. Just ask Blattner Brunner, Inc., a company that has renovated and moved into existing buildings five times in the past three decades. "We learned along the way that where you set up shop is extremely important," Joe Blattner explained. "And it's about more than just visibility. Your location can directly impact how you grow."

As we'll see in the pages to come, there are plenty of locations available in any setting that might make sense for your company. There are compelling reasons to move downtown in a city, where you can be closer to universities and the young talent they provide (to say nothing of the greater access to transportation and walkable activities and amenities). There are compelling reasons to move to the suburbs, where space is less expensive, parking is usually free, and your people with families might be more inclined to live. And there are compelling reasons to move to fringe markets, where you can get in on the buzz of an up and coming neighborhood while enjoying all the same advantages of downtown space, and usually at a slightly lower rent.

When choosing a location, what matters most in this modern market is cultural fit, accessibility, walkability, and yes, visibility. Out of respect for Lord Samuel's timeless wisdom, let's review those factors in reverse order.

VISIBILITY STILL MATTERS, BUT THE DEFINITIONS HAVE CHANGED

You can see the Bentley from I-376, Pittsburgh's busiest highway, the primary artery that delivers a hundred thousand cars from the south and west suburbs into the city, and also the fastest route from the airport to downtown. All those millions of people that pass it by each year are more aware of the Burns Scalo brand than they would have been otherwise. We could've put up a billboard (and we do advertise on billboards), but having that visibility from the highway is like a bigger, better, and *totally free* version of the same effort. I once asked someone if they've ever heard of Burns Scalo. "You mean the place in that great building off the highway?" was the reply. "*Everyone* has heard of Burns Scalo." Obviously that's the kind of thing you want to hear.

The Bentley ensures that we're visibly promoting our message merely by being an excellent example of the kinds of buildings we build and run. It also serves as an extraordinary recruiting tool for all those talented people stuck in traffic. "I could be working in that awesome building right now," at least a few of them think, "but instead I have to wait another twenty minutes to get through this tunnel so I can fight even more traffic downtown." This isn't a knock on downtown office space, either (downtown space is absolutely the most logical play for many businesses). Rather, the point is that, thanks to our impressive building and enviable visibility, our brand is on people's minds during their daily commute. That's a nice benefit. It's not essential to our success, but it's certainly a plus.

Another plus about being visible and so close to traffic is that it brings a ton of energy into the building. It's energizing to look out the window and see all those cars going by. At night, it's a genuinely beautiful light display. And all day, it helps give our staff and our recruits a sense that this place is where the action is. This is something that most people want. Look at New York City. Look at any major city in the world, for that matter. There's a reason so many millions of people are interested in packing themselves into those tight spaces: they favor living in places where there's a whole lot going on. It's not just about entertainment, either. There's a sense of belonging that comes from being adjacent to or surrounded by a bustling, vibrant place. The emotional impact is considerable.

But even with all these benefits, traditional visibility isn't as essential as it was in Lord Samuel's day simply because there are so many effective ways to be visible *without* having that on-site energy or the location that thousands and thousands of people can see each day. When they were building a new hockey arena in downtown Pittsburgh, many people were surprised when the sponsor was revealed to be Consol Energy. After all, Heinz and PNC sell directly to consumers, and their names grace the football and baseball stadiums, respectively. But with Consol, here's a company that sells coal and gas in a very regulated industry, and they don't sell it directly to the consumer. So why in the world would Consol want to pay all that money for the naming rights?

Visibility. Consol rightly recognized that a key portion of its workforce would soon need to be replaced by younger recruits. With their physical location in the south suburbs, they enjoyed less direct visibility with the thousands of graduating college kids downtown. If they were going to win any of the battles in the talent war, then they needed to make sure that, when the most talented of those kids received job offers from both Consol and PNC, they had a more difficult choice to make.

Before, it might've been a no-brainer: you take the job with the brand you recognize. But after the hockey arena, now Consol benefits from visibility and brand recognition on a more competitive level. Incidentally, the naming rights to the arena recently switched to PPG Paints, which represents a bit of a marriage between the Consol strategy and the more traditional consumer-product bent.

However you look at the question, the answer is the same. Having a great location *can* depend on visibility, but if you want visibility, you don't necessarily *need* a great location. Rather, you just need a strong branding effort. You need to do whatever it takes to become a household name so that you can enjoy enhanced public trust, better recruiting, and higher profits, as a result.

So, how do you do that? It starts by marrying the traditional location-benefit of visibility with new trends related to *accessibility* and *walkability*.

BE ACCESSIBLE. BE WALKABLE. WIN THE TALENT WAR.

If you're going to win the growing talent war, what *is* essential is that your business is accessible, and that it resides in an area that is walkable to the kinds of amenities and services your staff can use to help meet the work-life blend. The reasons are obvious: if it's genuinely difficult to get to your office, who would want to work there? And if you're a talented employee who receives a job offer at a place that is more convenient to access, why wouldn't you make the switch? On the walkability side, where would you rather work—a place that's in the middle of nowhere, where you have to drive to everything, or a place where you can park right behind the office, then walk to the daycare center, where you'll drop off your children before strolling over to the dry cleaner, the coffee shop, a retail location of your cell phone provider, your hair salon, and so on?

"Walkability, as it relates to an employer's location, will be one of the key factors that drives employment in the future," said Paul Griffith, Senior Managing Director with Newmark Knight Frank Valuation & Advisory (NKF). "In the coming years, we're going to see continued demand for office space in urban markets, particularly those with well-developed neighborhoods that provide ancillary services for office workers." Paul has seen these trends play out in many different markets in recent years, and based on NKF's feasibility and market studies, it seems clear that the trends are becoming the norm. "It's all culturally driven. Employers are seeking office space that has more of a neighborhood feel, where their employees can either live close by and walk or have easy access to public transportation and recreational and entertainment venues."

For some companies, locations that can meet all these needs reside in the kinds of mixed-use complexes sprouting up all over every suburb in America. For others, it makes better sense to check all these boxes with a downtown or fringe market location. Whatever the case, when it comes to recruiting, it's often best to locate your company near the talent you're looking to acquire.

Think about it this way: if you're a highly talented young person preparing for your first job after college or post-graduate studies, where are you going to start your search? Probably in places that you're already familiar with. One of those places is the city where you're attending college. And if you're the kind of job candidate who will be in high demand, your first choices are going to be with the brands you recognize (visibility). You'll then whittle those choices down based on how easy it will be for you to get from where you plan to live to where you plan to work (accessibility). Then, a huge factor in determining your final choice will be how much you like the amenities offered by the neighborhood where the physical office is located (walkability).

Put another way, if you're the employer, then visibility gets you a place in the battle, but it's accessibility and walkability that will win it for you. As a huge added benefit, accessibility and walkability will also contribute to a recruit's overall job satisfaction, which will keep him/her under your employ for longer.

Visibility, accessibility, and walkability: these are three of the deciding factors for any talented recruit, and so they must be the three primary factors to consider when choosing your location.

As we'll examine in the next section, employees under thirty years old increasingly tend to favor spaces that allow them quick and easy access to public transportation. Absent that, they prefer quick, low-traffic commutes that end in ample parking. So if you're currently located in a place where public transportation isn't available, and the commute for your target market of talent would be a long, miserable slog, then you're not in the right location.

Of course, not every company can promise a stress-free commute to every one of its employees, but if you're seeking top talent to replace a soon-to-be-retiring key staffer or workforce (and who isn't?), then step 1 is identifying where the largest number of your targeted talent lives, and step 2 is moving your office to a location that is easier for them to get to.

Next, walkability. How many work-life needs can your people meet by walking to them? How many perks does the surrounding neighborhood offer? I've mentioned the shops, services, and public transportation already, but the walkability picture goes beyond these elements. There is also the availability of quality housing in the area. There's no better commute, after all, than one you can take on foot. Then there are the restaurants, bars, retail space, hotels, and outdoor activities that will keep your people occupied and engaged when they're not in the office.

"The best locations on the walkability scale are the ones that offer synergy of use and homogeneity of purpose," Paul explained. "Can employees' living and social needs be met in the employer's neighborhood or via a convenient transportation system? Will they be surrounded by other people with similar work and lifestyle choices?"

In this way, walkability is an ease-of-use thing, but it's also a community and cultural thing. How naturally does your office space and the mission of the company it houses blend with the surrounding community? What are the opportunities for you to partner your culture with your neighbors' culture? How many like-minded companies are in this location? The more you fit culturally with the rest of the businesses in the location, the more opportunities you have to attract talent. The more your people fit socially with the other people living and working in the neighborhood, the more likely you are to retain them long-term.

Many of the amenities we have discussed up to this point can contribute to better walkability, as well. For instance, having a comfortable and engaging outdoor space outside your office goes a long way toward employee happiness and recruiting success. Efforts like incorporating a patio, providing access to walking trails, setting up bike racks or indoor bike storage, installing outdoor gaming, grilling, exercising, or meeting areas, and adding a rooftop deck make your business more walkable even if you're not in an area that already features these amenities, as it brings that need to connect with outdoor experiences closer.

Of course, when it comes to visibility, accessibility, and walkability, size of the company does matter. For large companies like Rice Energy, the most recent trends have been rather split. The larger among them (the Googles and Nikes of the world) are building huge campuses that incorporate all three elements of great location. Lately, we have seen a trend for more companies moving into downtown and fringe market areas so they can be closer to talented new recruits graduating from universities while also finding more natural fits in terms of accessibility (public transportation and easy access to housing) and walkability (other businesses and neighborhood synergies that help meet the work-life blend).

At the same time, some large companies and many mid-sized firms like Waldron Private Wealth are finding natural fits in the suburbs, where under-40 talent has been moving in droves so they can start families, where new construction is less costly, where parking is plentiful and usually free, and where the bar to meeting the visibility, accessibility, and walkability factors is lower.

For smaller companies—and particularly for those of the startup variety—the weight must fall heavier on commutes and distance to talent. For this reason, a large percentage of smaller companies tend to favor urban areas, where they can allow the surrounding neighborhoods and businesses to help meet the visibility, accessibility, and walkability factors all at once. But in the end, whatever the size of the company, synergies and homogeneous uses are the wave of the very near future. The perfect location is one that promises a comfortable, healthy workplace that enhances brand recognition, is easy to get to, fits well culturally with the surrounding neighborhood, and allows its employees the opportunity to meet many of their work-life needs on foot. It's all just a matter of *finding* that perfect location.

URBAN VS. SUBURBAN: FINDING A LOCATION TO MATCH YOUR CULTURE

For years, the primary question for any company trying to choose its location was, "What's the rent?" This sparked a decades-long focus in the commercial real estate industry for brokers to find ways to get the best "deal" for their clients. The location didn't matter quite as much as the bottom line cost. "Office space used to be a commodity," said Mark Popovich, Senior Managing Director with HFF, Inc., a company that provides capital markets and brokerage services to owners of commercial real estate. "The quality of the space was less important. Location factored into the decision, but it was really more about price."

If we look at recent history, that price-driven motivation has led to something of a rubber band effect as it relates to where companies have preferred to house themselves. "The central business district was still the place to be back in the 70s and 80s," Paul Griffith explained. "But then, in places like Detroit and Cleveland and Pittsburgh, the collapse of big industries is part of what led to the push for big companies to move to the suburbs. The appeal was pretty clear. You could get into something that was three to five stories high and not have to share a skyscraper with twenty other companies. There were these huge parking fields. And the suburbs started booming with amenities like restaurants and hotels."

In many cities in the 90s, the downtown areas were essentially dead. With all those businesses moving out of town, the residents moved along with them. But if you look at cities like Pittsburgh, the rubber band is snapping back. The revitalization of downtown areas and fringe markets is very real, and it all comes down to accessibility and walkability. While the suburbs had a lot going for them (and still do), it's just so much easier to promote a walkable work-life situation in a city, where all these amenities are already so tightly packed into the surrounding neighborhood.

"A lot more thought goes into walkability," Mark Popovich said. "That's a term you never heard ten years ago. Employers are much more sensitive to making their employees happy from a recruiting and retention standpoint. That has risen to the top. So it's more about amenities, what the location looks like, whether it's a sustainable space, whether it has a fitness center or access to outdoor activities, and so on. Today, these factors play a much more important role than price. And as brokers, we've had to rethink the way we approach the relationship with our clients. Rather than trying to be a hero by getting the price down, the goal should be to find the best fit for the company."

And as a personal aside, let's not forget that your rent is likely only 3% to 7% of your operating budget. It's not that you need to pay a huge amount more on the rent. We're really talking about an incidental cost increase here, and the result is that best fit Mark mentioned.

So, how do you find the best fit for your company? What matters most is how closely your location and your space reflects your organizational values and the message you're trying to send to your people and recruits. "A really nice space can make you feel better about everything," Mark said. "If you live in a nice home, you want to show it off. It's the same thing with your office. If you're in a great office, you're *proud* of it. And it makes you feel better because it tells you that your employer cares about your quality of life during the eight to ten hours you spend in the office every day."

"We also have to consider the changes to the way people work," he continued. "It used to be that if you worked for PwC, you went into the office. Staying home wasn't an option. Splitting time wasn't, either. Now that more people are able to do this, places like PwC have to think about ways to get their people into the office more often than not."

"On the demand side," Paul Griffith said, "studies we have recently completed have shown changes in what employers want for their employees. Whether you're in the city or the suburbs, you have to give them access to things they can't get at home. Employers are seeking buildings that incorporate outdoor space and amenities like rooftop decks, adjoining greenspace and trails, or even something as simple as bike racks.

"Then there are the suite-specific adaptations, where you're looking for a more open concept that allows people to work side by side, or a hoteling concept, where employees share or reserve space on a daily or weekly basis based on when they're going to be in the office. Amenities are the big piece. A well-designed café can make a huge difference for any company."

In many ways, the location you choose and the kind of space you design comes down to your identity as a company. "Small companies will be more cost-conscious by nature," Paul said. "Right against that, though, they're still looking at being able to attract and retain employees. That's where questions about commutes and proximity to amenities come into play. For bigger companies, it's mostly the same, because no matter where you set up, you need that walkability and access to amenities."

The Case for the City:

Of course the city's biggest advantage is that it features most of the visibility, accessibility, and walkability features we've been discussing, and they're baked right in. For a company that chooses to house itself in the city, there is less need to create spaces or opportunities to access the other elements of the work-life blend. Provided you pick the right location, those things are already there. Access to public transportation and proximity to young talent graduating or soon to be graduating from universities are huge benefits, as well.

The drawback to the city is of course always going to be space and cost. Downtown locations tend to come with higher rents for smaller spaces. Parking is often costly and sometimes difficult. And if you intend to construct a new space or renovate an existing one, the expense tends to be significantly higher.

That said, smaller companies tend to do well in cities. And lately, even some of the world's biggest companies are joining the fray. McDonald's is moving from its old location in suburban Oak Brook, IL into Chicago's West Loop, where they believe it will be easier for them to attract and keep top talent. Similarly, Reebok is constructing a beautiful new headquarters in Boston. Aetna is moving to Manhattan.[1] Why is this the case? If you're seeking talented young people, you set up shop in the city or near the colleges and universities.

Even companies that have established themselves in the suburbs for decades are pondering at least partial moves. Many advocate for keeping the suburban location for the home office while setting up a satellite space in the city. This helps recruit young talent with cultural preferences for urban locations and a lower desire to commute from downtown into the suburbs.

The concern from some decision-makers here is about the message it sends to the rest of the staff already working in the suburbs. The question is whether this flashy new space downtown somehow elevates the new hires above the existing employees. You combat that concern by making it clear that your culture is one that encourages the chance to self-define where you prefer to work. If a new hire wants to work in the urban location, he/she is welcome, and when the time comes that he/she would rather move out to the suburbs, as long as the position and space is open, he/she is welcome to make the move.

A strategy like this serves to make a company more agile, which is not to be confused with mobility and flexibility. Agile is all about allowing your company and your people to quickly pivot toward their needs. Think about Amazon, whose second home office will allow them to offer their new hires the chance to choose which coast to live on (while also offering their existing employees the benefit of being able to move from one home office to the other, should the need ever arise). It's an extraordinary and hugely disruptive advantage in the talent war to be able to tell your people and your recruits, "You can choose where you want to work, and if you want to move, as long as the position is available, just say the word and we'll help you move."

1 O'Connell, Jonathan. "As Companies Relocate to Big Cities, Suburban Towns Are Left Scrambling." The Washington Post. July 16, 2017.

The Case for the Suburbs:

Having read all that, you might assume that I believe suburban office parks to be a thing of the past. No, suburban office parks aren't dead. It's just that, to compete, they have to feel more like urban centers. They need to feature a comparable level of accessibility, visibility, and walkability. So as long as they're multi-use, they're fine. But if we're talking about one of those office parks that's just an office with some parking stuck out in the middle of nowhere, then yes, it's dead.

If we assume multi-use, though, the suburbs do have a few considerable advantages. Even though the current workforce is rapidly aging toward retirement, young people aren't the only talented potential employees out there. As I've been fond of pointing out, soon, 70% of the workforce will be in that 25-year-old to 40-year-old demographic. You might recognize that group as being the prime age to train for and assume leadership roles. You might also recognize those as the prime ages for settling down and starting a family. And what happens when a person settles down and starts a family? Well, at least by the time they're ready for their second child, they typically start to think about all the advantages of the suburbs. You can get a bigger house for less money. There's more space out there, so you're far more likely to find a home with a big yard. It's cheaper and easier to own and park a car. The schools tend to be better funded. There's wider access to outdoor activities and youth sports.

From an employer's perspective, all these same factors apply. On top of that, setting up shop in the suburbs makes the commute for those family-starting employees that much easier, as they no longer have to fight the bridge and tunnel traffic.

The big problems are those accessibility and walkability components. In a traditional suburban office park, you're usually looking at an outdated building that isn't terribly close to upscale housing and retail shops. If it's closer to the highway, it tends to be further from outdoor activities and sports facilities, as well. This is exactly why you're seeing so many new commercial construction projects featuring mixed-use elements. Office complexes that are strictly for work and nothing else are going the way of the dinosaur. Huge complexes complete with combinations of office space, restaurant and retail locations, and luxury apartment and townhouse complexes are popping up everywhere. The effort here is to create a city-like experience with all those same benefits of suburban living. It is a have-your-cake-and-eat-it-too approach to attracting twenty-to-forty-somethings moving to the suburbs.

Lockheed Martin and Marriott International recently moved into a similar location in suburban Bethesda after long searches for appropriate inner-city spaces.[2] Suburban development isn't dead, but the future for these business parks is that they have to have the amenities and walkable outlets nearby. The goal is to find ways to make the suburban park function more like an urban park. Enjoy trading the $300-per-month parking for the free parking, and while you're at it, enjoy this rotating series of food trucks. Move to where you can have that yard and garage, and we'll still give you the Pilates classes in our fitness center. You've spent your years of lower expenses by enjoying the downtown nightlife and cultural scene, but now that it's time for a mortgage, we'll bring you similar social and cultural opportunities like happy hours in the lounge, movie screenings and live concerts, and a sand volleyball court—all at a price that's affordable for a working family.

SO…WHERE SHOULD YOU SET UP SHOP?

Urban or suburban—it's all a question of knowing yourself. What are the products or services you're selling? What is the current state of your brand? What does the ideal candidate for your open positions look like? What neighborhood, suburb, or geographic area does that ideal candidate think is hot right now? All these answers and more contribute to the definition of the market that's best suited for your office space.

Of course it's more than just educated guesswork. "You have to understand the market you're trying to enter," Paul Griffith explained. "What are the markets and neighborhoods people are attracted to right now? How walkable is the location? And don't overlook homogeneity of the area. In other words, are there a lot of like-minded businesses nearby? This is important, because it makes the kinds of partnerships and share of information that leads to growth more natural."

2 Spivack, Miranda S. "The Old Suburban Office Park Is Getting a Big Reboot." The New York Times. December 5, 2017.

DELTA POINT:
IF YOU RENT IT

I'm sure you recognized the play on the iconic statement from Field of Dreams that serves as this chapter's title. Of course the statement, "If you build it, they will come" had several layers of deeper meaning in the movie, but from a purely financial perspective, it meant that Kevin Costner's character, Ray Kinsella, had to take the leap and spend the money on creating his baseball diamond in his corn field and then just trust that people would show up and pay to see it. There's a similar (albeit far, far less risky) leap behind choosing your location and upgrading your office space. First, you need to identify where your talent resides, and then you need to trust that if you rent a dynamic space, it will help bring that talent in.

Fortunately, just like in Field of Dreams, this strategy is almost supernaturally effective. In every industry. And in every location you could possibly choose (assuming you choose well by renting a place with visibility, accessibility, and walkability in a location that's close to where your target talent wants to live and work). If you take the leap and spend the money on researching and scouting the right location, and if you commit to that small delta of increase in the tiny portion of your operating budget that is your rent, that extra investment will pay for itself quickly. In fact, many of the best companies we have worked with at Burns Scalo find that their investment is returned to them in terms of talent inside of one year, and in terms of productivity inside of three years.

Finding yourself in a popular neighborhood is always a good thing, but so is moving into a neighborhood where you can borrow some of the brand equity of larger companies. Occupying the same space as a larger employer with a positive reputation sends a strong message to your existing employees and future recruits. Further, as your company grows, you may be able to attract some talented people from the big company who might be interested in joining something a little closer to the ground floor.

If you're running a mid-sized or an otherwise growing company, reaching that next level can sometimes hinge on your proximity to mass transit, colleges, and the airport. For some, moving the entire company into such a location might be too costly. In these cases, sometimes it is best practice to establish a smaller hub-location.

Consider housing one of the more exciting and younger elements of your company in a space closer to the nearest urban university, for example, and this could help heighten your visibility while allowing some of your key employees to enjoy the accessibility and walkability factors at a fraction of the cost. If you don't have the budget for the rent in a full satellite location, coworking and shared offices like WeWork[3] have lately become the rage. These high-end office spaces rent out workspace like hotel rooms or apartments on a monthly basis. In this way, you get all the access to modern, exceptional amenities and space without committing to a more permanent move for all or some of your people.

Satellite locations are potential game-changers for a number of reasons. Large companies sometimes house their management positions in a premium location, for example, while placing the rest of the operation in a less costly space. They also help with recruiting in varied locations. A growing company can only suck so much of the labor force out of a single geographic area, after all, so establishing a presence in multiple places can help keep the talent running high and the new ideas flowing in from different corners of the city, region, state, or country.

The absolute final step—and it really shouldn't be anywhere near a deciding factor—is cost. As I've mentioned, these decisions shouldn't be cost-driven, or you run the risk of hindering your culture and your productivity in favor of saving a few bucks on rent. Or, as Mark Popovich said, "It's time to stop thinking about these deals as transactions and start thinking about them as strategies for attracting and keeping top talent, enhancing productivity, and improving culture. Good real estate makes good businesses better."

---

3 https://www.wework.com/

The goal should not be to find the cheapest space in either the city or the suburbs, but rather, to find the space that offers the best possible blend of walkability to amenities, accessibility to transportation and housing, and visibility to your audience of potential talent and customers.

Ultimately, that is the closing message on location. Yes, the rules have changed, and yes, they are slightly different depending on the size and growth trajectory of your company. But at the end of the day, it is all about investing in a visible, accessible, and walkable office space that will improve the lives of your people, enhance productivity, and attract more talent. Ask anyone who's done this and they will tell you the same: once you move to a dynamic office space, you'll never look back.

PART 2:
PRODUCTIVITY

THE MOST
PRECIOUS
COMMODITY
IS TIME.

CHAPTER 5

LEVERAGING TIME, SPACE, AND EXPERIENCE

"Time has more value than money.
You can get more money, but you cannot get more time."
- Jim Rohn

As great business leaders, we recognize the drive to maximize the return on every investment we make in our companies. But too few of us see our office space for what it truly is: an incredible opportunity to leverage Return on Time, Return on Space, and Return on Experience into ultimate productivity.

It all starts with the typical debate on how modern companies are rethinking the workday. I could point out how the 9-to-5 shift has become something of a dinosaur—a relic from the Industrial Revolution, when the world's best innovators decided that the twenty-four-hour day should be split evenly between eight hours of work, eight hours of leisure, and eight hours of sleep. I mean, how long has it been since *that* was still true? I can't remember the last time I felt like I had eight hours to spend completely on myself and my family, let alone the last time I had eight whole hours of sleep.

I could cite how 43% of employed Americans perform at least some of their work from a place other than the office, or how people who spend 100% of their workday at the office report the same levels of engagement as people who spend 100% of their workday in a remote location.[1] But what really matters is the answer to these two questions: What was the last thing you did before going to sleep last night? And what was the first thing you did when you woke up?

If your typical day looks anything like mine, the answer to both questions is, "I responded to my work emails and texts." Usually, I haven't even rolled out of bed yet before I start tapping messages into

1 "State of the American Workplace." Gallup Poll, February, 2017. http://news.gallup.com/reports/199961/7.aspx.

Photo: The Beacon – Architectural design by Pfaffmann + Associates.

my phone. It used to be that work was like a light switch. You switched it on when you got into the office in the morning and you switched it off at the end of the day. Now, it's more like a volume knob. It's always on; you just turn it up or down depending on where you are and what you're doing.

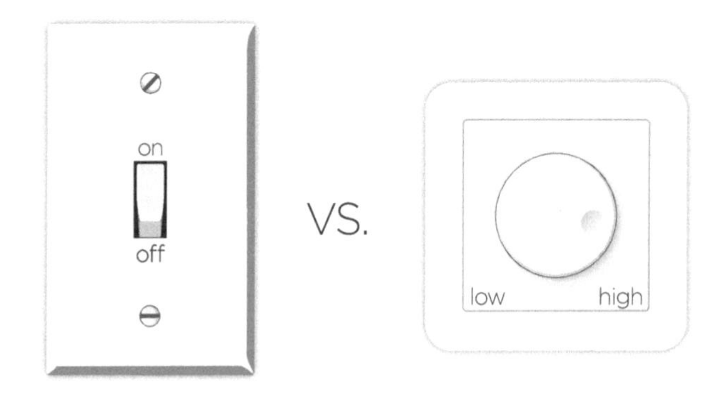

There are many reasons why this volume knob revolution is happening, but they aren't just related to technology. Yes, we have our computers, our phones, our wearable tech, our AI assistants, our fully networked homes, and our more secure remote bridges to work, and they're all helping ensure that we're able to connect to our work more seamlessly. But what's more interesting—particularly as it relates to commercial office space—is that all this technology has stirred a *cultural* change related to how we think about work. As most jobs have become less physically demanding and more mentally demanding, and with more people recognizing that you don't necessarily need to be physically present at the office to do them, we're starting to question the work-life blend in a way we haven't had to since back when the Titans of Industry were still calling the shots. So, what *would* Henry Ford do, anyway?

THE SCREENAGER EFFECT

Over the course of the past couple decades, that volume knob has led to a greater expectation of work-connectedness for both the employer and employee. When I first started running Burns Scalo, it was still the light switch. The norm was that everyone came into work at 8 or 9, worked hard for eight to ten hours, and then headed home. Except for rare occasions, my employees and I wouldn't contact each other on our home phones to discuss work in the evenings, the early mornings, or on weekends. Today, though, when I send an email or text, no matter what time of day or night it is, I know that the recipient will receive the notification on his or her phone instantaneously. Depending on where they've set their volume knob, I might hear back right away, or it might take a little longer, but the odds are pretty good that I'll get a response before 9am on Monday. It helps that we pay for their phone and data plans, and also that we provide them with laptops and tablets that they are welcome (and encouraged) to take home. Benefits like these tend to compel our people to pay more attention to work in traditional non-working hours.

Everywhere—all across the planet and in every industry—employers are leaning on many of their people to remain connected and available while they're at home. Every year, technological and cultural changes allow people to spend more time and attention on work. And as a result, some industries are looking not just at the costs of absenteeism, burnout, disengagement, and turnover that we've been discussing to this point, but they've also been dealing with a dramatic drag on productivity.

There are two potential fixes to the productivity problem, but only one of those fixes is realistic in most industries. We could accept that we have to allow our employees to unplug when they're not at work. This is the less realistic fix, given that this same culture of constant connectedness has led most of the consumers we serve to expect 24/7 access to the people who supply and support their products and services. If our customers need to be able to reach us at any time, then we need our employees to be there for them at any time.

Also, most employees don't actually *want* to disconnect from work. In fact, according to a recent Gallup poll, 79% of workers across a wide variety of industries viewed the idea of being able to work remotely after business hours in an at least somewhat positive light.[2] Whether it's technological advancements or Millennial preferences, we appear to be living and working in a culture where most people think that constant connectedness is more than just something they have to do to

2 "Most U.S. Workers See Upside to Staying Connected at Work." Jim Harter, Sangeeta Agrawal, Susan Sorenson. Gallup News. April 30, 2014.

keep their jobs. It has become standard practice. People are mixing personal and business life into the full 24/7. Most people of working age, but particularly Millennials, are always connected to their work, to their friends, and to their social media, and so they don't just *accept* the idea that they must always be on call; they *expect* to always be on call. And Generation Z's working-age members aren't old enough to even remember a time before the constant connection between work and life. I call them "Screenagers," due to their all-encompassing relationship with screens. This is how they've lived all their lives.

This is a huge part of why the other potential fix makes so much more sense: there has to be some give and take here. From a cultural perspective, it's a matter of understanding that if they're giving you more of their personal time so they can get work done, then you need to be okay with allowing them to attend to personal matters during traditional working hours. A huge part of happiness in this new work-life blend is being able to communicate with family and friends at any time, as well.

Just like that volume knob for work, there's a volume knob for the personal life. The way we connect with people is never really switched off. We just turn it up or down. Really, how can we expect people to ignore their home or social lives while they're in the office when they can't really help how all those texts, emails, chats, and social media messages pop up on their screens automatically? If at night we expect a mix of business and personal, then we need to start being okay with having a similar mix at the office. Shifting toward this culture improves morale and the sense of community at work, and also makes your people that much more willing to put in some productive work time while they're not in the office.

This effort works from a pure office space perspective, as well. If more of our employees are dedicating more of their time to completing their work while they're traditionally supposed to be at leisure, then the best way to return the favor—and the best way to get the highest level of productivity in return for your investment in their salaries—is to make the workplace feel more inviting, more appealing, and more like home. In fact, ideally, the goal should be to provide a workplace that is even *more* luxurious than home. Most people spend more of their conscious time at work than in their houses, after all.

We want to get to where we're providing the best possible vibe and experience in the workplace. "Vibe" refers to how the space makes you feel, while "experience" is that feeling that makes you want to come back every day. If we're looking at blurrier lines between leisure and work time at home, then we owe it to our employees to blur them in the workplace by way of vibe and experience, as well.

FLEXIBILITY ISN'T ENOUGH

It's time to recognize that simply asking our employees to park themselves at their desks for eight hours a day isn't going to guarantee optimal productivity. That technology that allows for constant connection doesn't just stop distracting people while they're sitting at their desks, after all. And even if you restrict access to social media or personal phone use, the average employee still loses a ton of time to unproductive meetings, unnecessary or inefficient work emails, and distractions from other employees. This is how eight hours at the office almost never equates to anywhere near eight hours of actual productivity. To get to the highest possible Return on Time, the best employers are finding ways to ensure a better blend of work and leisure at the office, so that their employees can feel more dedicated to giving their work the attention it needs at whatever hours of the day they are most productive.

You might be telling yourself that you've heard these arguments before, since they are in fact the impetus for the flex work schedule. But what the best leaders are realizing is that a flexible schedule isn't enough on its own. You might intend for the message to be, "Life happens. We're still measuring results, of course, but if you have to take some time off because of something in your life, then go ahead and take the time. Just make sure you get the job done." Unfortunately, the way many employees interpret a flexible schedule is that you're requiring them to work longer hours in exchange for the freedom to occasionally duck out during the traditional workday. This is why so many people in flexible work environments wind up putting in the usual 9-to-5 before taking work home with them every night. Given this trend, it should come as no surprise that while flex schedules are helpful in employee recruitment, they don't tend to cut down on burnout and turnover.

So if technology and culture is allowing you to *ask* more of your people, then the solution is to *give* more in return. Simply offering a flexible schedule won't cut it. To maximize your Return on Time, you have to *show* them how much you value the work they do for you, both at home and in the office. The term used to be "family-friendly employer," referencing that you recognize how family needs to come first, but the better term today is "life-friendly employer." As a culture, the things we value in life have changed, extending beyond the family to a host of other people and factors. To be life-friendly, our job as leaders and decision-makers is to ensure that the office and its culture are at least every bit as comfortable, and ideally, every bit as engaging, healthy, productive, and even enjoyable as our people's home lives.

If we can find ways to make our people happy while at work, then we improve the way they use the time they dedicate to their jobs. So, how do we make our employees happy at work? A flexible schedule is one component, but to differentiate ourselves from the competition, improve corporate culture, and maximize our Return on Time, we have to give *more*. Our workplace amenities contribute a great deal more to these factors than many decision-makers realize. Employers that provide easy access to effective workspaces for individual work and focused stations for collaboration see a 22% improvement in productivity. And after promoting wellness initiatives, 25% of companies see an improvement in retention and 47% enjoy an improvement in employee engagement.[3]

The reason for these productivity gains is simple: people work better when they are happier and have their needs met. But keep in mind, also, that you aren't the only person in the equation concerned with the Return on Time. These same technological and cultural changes we've been discussing throughout the chapter also directly impact your people's access to time. In more ways than one, time is the ultimate commodity.

In a world where there is more information and more potential for obligation, entertainment, and distraction than anyone could possibly meet in a single day, people tend to appreciate convenience. They want a place where they can have more than one of their needs met at the same

3 Various authors. "Better Business Performance Through Better Workspace Performance: Designing the Workplace Experience." A CBRE Thought Series. CBRE, Inc. 2016.

time. Think about your local fitness mega-center. What used to be just a place to exercise now has a childcare facility, a café, and a juice bar built right in. When people have a hard enough time finding a whole hour to exercise, they very much appreciate being able to save the time it would otherwise take to drop off their children at a separate daycare facility, grab their morning smoothie, or pick up something to take to work for lunch or home for dinner.

Your office space puts you in a unique position to meet multiple needs better and more efficiently than anyone else can. Find ways to integrate work, wellness, personal services, and leisure into your office space, and your people will pay you back with a drastic increase in productivity. Help them save time, and they will be far more likely to give that time to work. As a huge added benefit, people who have their needs met are much more *productive* while they're working. They won't just have more time to give you; you'll get more return on the time they give.

RETURN ON SPACE

This brings us to the "how" portion of the show. The way to maximize time and productivity is to remember that commercial office space is an underutilized tool in the capitalist toolbox. If we use our office space as a means to show our employees that we care about them, then they will care more about the success of the business. In a world of self-interest, the best leaders find ways to ensure that their people's interests are aligned with the company's. With better, more efficient, more sustainable, more inspiring, and more engaging workplaces, those interests align, and we *all* win.

Over the years, the standard corporate setting has seen quite an evolution. Closed-door offices gave way to the more efficient use of space offered by the cubicle design. The corresponding drain on productivity and culture that came with stale, factory-produced cubicles sparked a return to more variable workspace settings. But even now, as the trend moves toward open-plan flexibility, too many office designs fail to take full advantage of the available space. The trouble is that not nearly enough decision-makers recognize how active and collaborative work has become.

To foster the most efficient and effective work, we need to strike a balance between maximum productivity at the desk, ease of access to collaborative space, and adequate space for leisure, dining, and interdisciplinary crosstalk. The more comfortable your people are at their desks, the better their work product. The easier it is for them to collaborate effectively, the better your teams perform. And the more opportunities we provide for the people from HR to share ideas with the people from marketing, or the people from sales to share ideas with the people from R&D, the more spontaneous innovation will arise. As a benefit, as we focus on ensuring comfort and wellness across all these varied settings, it begins to attract and retain employees from a more diverse set of preferences and backgrounds.

In keeping with that theme, it is important to remember that the best designs recognize that there is no one-size-fits-all approach. Some people work better in teams, and some people work better individually. Not everyone responds best to open-plan layouts. Just encouraging open communication between employees does not guarantee that you are being ultimately efficient with your use of space. Ideally, that notion of flexibility should extend beyond time and into your space, as well. Yes, shared desks and bench seating can get people talking and moving around more often, but some people, and some tasks, benefit from the ability to find privacy (at least once in a while).

The goal, in other words, should not be to just cram as many people into the space as possible; rather, it should be to find ways to maximize productivity for each worker while also better utilizing the space you have so that it can meet multiple needs. Movable partitions, glass walls, alternative seating like sofas or café tables, temporary private offices, huddle rooms and phone rooms, and non-work spaces like cafés, fitness centers, or game rooms—all of these concepts can contribute to a better sense of adaptability, and make your workspace more agile in its effort to meet a variety of needs. In this way, you enhance an employee's ability to craft his or her space to a personal preference, and that ability leads to greater comfort and higher productivity. Additionally, by demonstrating your desire to give your people options that will help them suit their individual needs, each employee will more authentically connect with the success of your business. Show that you are buying into them, and they will buy into you.

RETURN ON EXPERIENCE

Most employers recognize that their employees derive happiness from more than one source. Yes, it is important to ensure that everyone can be comfortable and confident in their ability to do the job; and it is good to recognize that people tend to feel more fulfilled when they have opportunities to advance their careers and truly make a difference at work; but there are three other contributors to happiness at work that often go overlooked.

An employee's experience extends well beyond the job to which he or she is assigned. There is also the social aspect, and the needs here are best met when each employee has the opportunity to do more than just work alongside his or her coworkers. Social happiness at work comes from genuine connection to coworkers and a sense of belonging within the company. Then there is entertainment. When everything is all work and no play, you wind up with a whole lot of dull employees. People need to be able to escape once in a while—and this isn't just Millennial stuff either. Feeling comfortable at the office improves productivity on a level that demanding harder work or greater focus never could. As we'll cover in more detail in the next chapter, a happy employee is a productive employee.

Every great space, however it is designed, allows the people who work there to meet all these needs as efficiently and consistently as possible. But how do we get there? How do we ensure that we keep people engaged at their desks, fulfilled by their opportunities to make a difference, connect with their coworkers on a more authentic level, and genuinely enjoy being at work? We'll be digging deeper into the answers to this question in the chapters to come, but for now, consider these four equations for a better Return on Experience:

1. Amenities + Shared Experience = Belonging

   Think about where you made most of your friends. Did you meet them randomly on the street, and then grow the friendship from there? Or did you bond over a shared experience or community? It's likely your best friends are people you met at work, at the coffee shop, at the fitness center, on a social sports team, in a professional or social organization, and so on. This is because abiding friendship requires a sense of belonging, and of that bond that can only come from community and shared experience.

This is a huge part of why amenities are so much more than just a Millennial fad. Amenities create an authentic sense of belonging for employees. If you work in a place where all you have is a desk and an expectation to do your job, then the relationships you form with other people at work tend to be shallower. These other people are just a means to help you get your work done. But if you add amenities that people value, then you give them opportunities to bond over shared experience and a greater sense that they belong to the organization that provides them these perks.

You're more likely to form a genuine friendship with someone you see every morning as you take your children to the same on-site daycare or wait in line for your morning coffee in the lobby café. Your social interaction with another person is more rewarding and authentic over a meal in the café or outside at a food truck than it is in a conference call conducted across the table from each other in a conference room. You're more likely to actually enjoy another person's company if you've had opportunities to grab a drink in the nearby bar or exercise together in the office fitness center.

There are three amenity opportunities here, and they all spark a greater sense of comradery and belonging among your staff. The first is what you can construct, like a café or a coffee bar or a patio. The second is digital, or all those ways you can connect your people using the latest technology. The third is services. Every chance you give your staff to bump into each other at the daycare, while dropping off the dry cleaning, or waiting for their cars to be washed, the broader their shared experiences, and the more authentic their relationship becomes.

Create an environment that fosters better friendships at work, and morale rises, culture enhances, and productivity soars.

2. Luxury + Amenities = Positive Vibes

Here we have commercial office space taking a page out of the book of the hospitality industry. What can you remember about the best hotel you ever stayed in? If you're like me, the things that spring to mind are the amenities and the luxury. Great hotels commit to these elements for good reason: if you're extremely comfortable, and you're a little awed by the luxury, then you're far more likely to enjoy your stay, repeat that stay at a later date, and recommend the hotel to others. This impression of luxury leads to the most productive outcome they can hope for. Incidentally, this is why many hotels go to greater expense to enhance their lobbies over their guest rooms: that *first* impression goes a long way.

Also, most of these first-impression investments are low-cost and high-impact. They're exactly the kinds of investments all great business leaders look to make. With a high-end coffeemaker or a popcorn machine in the lobby, a hotel spends an insignificant amount of money while significantly heightening the customer experience (and as a nice benefit, it always smells nice when you first walk into the lobby). These same amenities make great sense for your office space, as well. And they are only the beginning. There are so many amenities that can be low-cost, high-impact. Construct outdoor walking trails. Put in a patio with a grill. Have a ping-pong table. Paint a shuffleboard surface in a hallway. Investments like these are low, one-time costs that can deliver on your investment for virtually forever.

A focus on luxury leads to greater productivity in the workplace, as well. Thinking like a hotel can take you a long way. Customer service, design aesthetic, personal employee perks, dry cleaning services, concierge services, and so on—these drive a sense of luxury, and the employee experience flourishes as a result. To receive ultimate productivity from a staff, the goal should be to project that same vibe and offer a similar experience through your design and amenities as any luxury hotel.

3. Interaction + Intelligent Use of Space = Agility

The companies that enjoy continual growth tend to be those that are most agile. When the market shifts, they are in best position to revise their strategies and move quickly to take advantage of new trends. These companies don't get there by accident. They get there by fostering as much interaction as possible between their employees on all levels.

This is a huge part of why companies that design office spaces that foster more authentic relationships, collaboration, and the sharing of ideas tend to be more innovative and adaptive. If your space allows for people from different departments and roles to interact, then these people tend to spot opportunities, as well as flaws in strategy, well in advance. Good things happen when people have chances to run into each other in shared spaces. They're more creative in these settings, and believe it or not, just having the chance to talk face to face increases productivity dramatically.

4. Efficiency + Comfortable Space = Productivity

If you've ever visited the National Air and Space Museum in Washington, D.C., you might have noticed how much care went into every design element of the spaceships the US first sent into orbit and to the moon. The interiors of those craft were shockingly intricate and remarkably ingenious. They had to be, given that the scientists involved had to figure out how to keep these astronauts alive and as comfortable as possible in incredibly tiny spaces. When you're only working with ten or twenty square feet of space, you have to make sure that every object in the room can do more than one thing, or be moved and reused in another way with efficiency. On top of that, every calculation about light, temperature, air quality, food and waste management, and so on, had to be absolutely perfect, or lives would be at risk.

These days, office design works much the same way, albeit without all the life-threatening scenarios. Studies are showing that the more multi-use spaces a workplace offers, the more employees interact, and the more productive their work becomes. Similarly, great lighting, better temperature regulation, and higher quality air lead directly to improvements in productivity. Thanks to more thoroughly networked and advanced technologies, it is possible to control all these elements in the office as completely (and even more efficiently) as on the space shuttle.

THE SECRET SAUCE

Before we move forward, let's revisit a central point from chapter 1—or the secret sauce, as it were. Everything we've been discussing in this book is about the people, not the real estate. The real estate is just the byproduct. Our goals as business leaders include providing sincere leadership, promoting an active culture, and creating a great office space in a great location that leads to great results. If we achieve these goals, then we start attracting and retaining the best people. We start demonstrating the health of our organization. We start showing that we're poised to be a winner in the future of business.

The best way to project these positive images is to do what the world's best companies are doing (and not just the tech companies, but places like McDonald's, Caterpillar, Reebok, and on and on). These companies aren't moving into inspiring new buildings just because they have money to burn. They're doing it because they recognize that winning in business is all about treating your people well so that they will treat your business well.

DELTA POINT:
THE WOW FACTOR MAKES MONEY

Now, with all of this in mind, I can take a wild guess that your thoughts have drifted back toward the expense. Amenities, luxury, redesign of space, modern light, temperature, and air quality controls—these things cost money. This is true. But again, we're never going to be talking about a scenario where you're paying $0 in rent. If your rent is currently 5% of your operating budget, and your payroll is 50%, then what does a few hundred or even a few thousand extra dollars a month on the rent matter if it's contributing so completely to improving employee happiness, loyalty, and productivity? Recall that 3-30-300 model from JLL,[4] and consider the data from CBRE that shows the competitive advantages of how dynamic spaces reduce absenteeism, healthcare costs, and recidivism while also increasing productivity.[5] In short, if you increase that small percentage of your operating budget by even 20%, the returns you can expect will far exceed the added expense.

In this way, the Wow Factor doesn't just cost money, it also makes money, and the money it makes tends to far outweigh the money it costs. Yes, keeping your expenses in check is important in any business, but we have to consider the weight we're placing on these expenses. At the end of the day, cost per square foot is so much less important than productivity per square foot, and making that investment in time, space, and experience is a sure way to boost the latter.

---

4 http://www.us.jll.com/united-states/en-us/services/corporates/consulting/reduce-real-estate-costs
5 Ibid.

TEAMWORK
Community
COWORKING
THINK
relax!
MOTIVATION
flexible
SOCIAL
Business

CHAPTER 6

WORK HAPPY

"Fifteen years ago, the Internet was an escape from the real world. Now the real world is an escape from the Internet."
- Noah Smith

In case it hasn't become obvious by now, I'm a guy who appreciates axioms. My staff will tell you that I throw them around all the time. These little nuggets of wisdom are always showing up in conversation, in company-wide emails, and in the messaging we share with clients. The first reason I love axioms is because it never hurts to borrow a little credibility from people who are wiser than me. But the main reason is this: nothing in the world sends a message quite like a statement that is undeniably *true*. That's a huge part of why the quote at the start of this chapter is one of my new favorites. You want to think about how productivity has changed over the past fifteen years? Just think about how your relationship with the Internet today compares to the way it was when you first started logging on. For instance, remember when it was called "logging on?" That seems like a lifetime ago.

What's really funny is that if you think back fifteen years, as Noah Smith invites us to, the Internet was more than just a distraction; it was also an *enticement*. In an effort to get your business, Internet providers used to champion the "blazing fast DSL speeds" they were now able to offer in your neighborhood. On the professional side, employers used to promise high-speed Internet as a means to attract talented new hires. In other words, back then, the Internet was an *amenity*. Right around the time when employers started realizing this fact, the wheat began separating from the chaff. Those who were first to embrace a vision of the future that included a ubiquitous Internet quickly became the world's top companies.

And this wasn't even the first time this sort of thing happened. Thirty to thirty-five years ago, the first major disruption to the way we work came in the form of the affordable personal computer. Fifteen years ago, it was high speed Internet. So if you're keeping score, every fifteen years or so, something comes along to completely disrupt our productivity at work. Today, we are very much in the midst of the latest disruption. Just like back when computers and the Internet were considered luxuries, the amenities offered in offices with the Wow Factor are very much changing the game for companies all over the world. Just like computers and the Internet, the reasons for this game-change are simple. Amenities are not entitlements; they're a means to keep people *happy,* and if people are *happy,* they're more productive.

That's a graphic we circulate to our staff at Burns Scalo Real Estate, and one we now hang on the wall in a place where everyone can see it. We believe in that message so deeply that we even employ someone with the official title of "Happiness Chief." The purpose of this role is to greet and provide for everyone who enters the building in a way that brightens their day. Our Happiness Chief is cheerful all the time, keeping that campfire burning for our cultural philosophies by always looking for ways to make the office a more enjoyable and engaging place.

That's our corporate philosophy in a nutshell, and it's the philosophy we reinforce with every amenity in our building and service we offer our staff. Why? First, because encouraging people to enjoy themselves is the right thing to do. And second, happy people do better, more effective *work.*

DELTA POINT:
WORKING ENGAGEMENT

Getting to that higher level of productivity is a matter of ensuring that your people are as engaged as often, as intensely, and for as long as possible while at the office. According to the Hay Group, companies with highly engaged employees outperform those with disengaged employees by 89% in customer satisfaction and an astonishing *400%* in revenue growth.[1]

So how do we keep our employees engaged to the point where we can hit these remarkable productivity numbers? The short answer is by leveraging our office space in ways that heighten employee happiness. The longer answer is that a focus on every employee's *wellness* is the surest means to make them happier. The more people who feel like all their needs are being met, they're stimulated by the environment, and they're *comfortable* at their workspaces, the more productive your staff will be.

When we look at the overall wellness picture, we're looking at ensuring proper ergonomics, appropriate lighting, great acoustics, thermal comfort, fresh air, healthy food, access to exercise, and opportunity to interact creatively and socially. Recent studies by JLL suggest that, regardless of age, employee productivity increases by as much as 6% for each of the above factors you optimize.[2] Better lights equals a 6% rise in productivity. Flexible, programmable temperature control jumps you up another 6%. Exercise is another 6%. You get the idea. And these are just the averages. Depending on your unique situation, some factors could increase productivity more than others.

---

1 Goffee, Rob and Jones, Gareth. "Creating the Best Workplace on Earth." Harvard Business Review. May 2013.
2 Various Authors. "Green + Productive Workplace." JLL.

YOUR COMPETITION IS ALREADY THINKING ABOUT THIS

If any of this sounds too Millennial for your taste, keep in mind that the competition is thinking about this stuff already. "Health and wellness is a major trend in the corporate sphere," said Pete Jefferson, Principal at BranchPattern, a building consultancy with a mission of improving life through better built environments. "Landlords are looking at things like the air quality and thermal comfort they provide to their tenants. Employers are seeking active design and more health-focused amenities. There's still a subset of facilities management groups that prefer an out of sight, out of mind approach—if I can't see it, it's not my problem. So this is still a competitive advantage. But more and more tenants are starting to care about these things, so it won't be long before they become mainstream."

For those who do pay attention to the wellness movement, they're starting to see extraordinary increases in productivity for every environmental element they optimize. "The research reveals that, as humans, we were designed to move," Pete explained. "That's where active design comes in. But just as important is the need to be connected to our surroundings."

As BranchPattern explains it, if occupants are subjected to monotonous spaces for an extended duration, then human physiology starts to kick in. The body starts to send signals to tell the brain that they are still working. For example, after sitting in a space with the same temperature for an extended duration, the thermal receptor network might send a signal to the brain expressing discomfort. While we might look toward HVAC systems and air temperature as the culprit, in reality, lack of movement may have been the more significant factor.

"If you're constantly surrounded by roses," Pete said, "then after a while, you stop smelling them. If we want spaces to be perceived as comfortable and human-centered, we have to move and have multi-sensory experiences in a variety of spaces." This illustrates a scientific concept called *alliesthesia*. In simplest terms, it is the experience of obtaining sensory pleasure due to variations in the environment. We experience this every time we feel a strong breeze on a hot day, or when we walk into a warmer building on a cold winter day.

How this applies to office space design is quite simple: you can't just throw in some potted plants and some new artwork and call it a day. The design needs to be focused on keeping people active—getting them up from their desks and seeking out varied spaces to work over the course of the day. It might sound counterintuitive to suggest that making people change the places where they work would increase productivity. After all, every time they have to carry their laptops from one place to another, those are lost minutes of potential work time, right? But the human mind benefits from the chance to refresh once in a while. That lost time in transit gets made up in spades once the brain has a chance to hit the reset button on surrounding stimuli.

Playing off that theme, there's a reason that just *going outside* is so refreshing. Human beings benefit from that connection to the natural world, and when they're actually in it, they're more creative, productive, and their moods elevate. With this in mind, the best designs don't just keep staffs moving around, but make them feel more connected to the outside world.

"It starts with getting the thermal comfort basics right," Pete said. "And we want people not only moving, but also going through different sensory experiences as they move. We're trying to create spaces that respond to how human physiology is designed to function, so we mimic the experiences that we evolved to function in. The natural world provides us with different temperatures in different spaces; variability in air flows; and we get visible connections to the sky and what's happening outside. The more you can *see* outside while still feeling thermally comfortable, the more you connect to that comfortable sensation of shelter."

Give your people the opportunity to be stimulated by varied environments inside while also connecting them to sightlines to the outside. Do this, and the office starts to feel not just more comfortable, but more like *home*. Keeping them comfortable and meeting their needs in terms of their physical environment keeps them more engaged in work, and also more satisfied with their surroundings and feeling as if they have greater *ownership* of the space. When it starts to feel like home, they start to care more about it. And when they care more about it, everything improves—culture, productivity, respect for the space and for each other, and general happiness and wellbeing.

QUALITY SPACE, QUALITY WORK

So if we know that wellness leads to happiness and happiness leads to productivity, and we know that a host of environmental factors are increasingly connected to the overall wellness picture, then what are the environmental factors we should be paying attention to? In a nutshell, it all comes down to the elements that we see, feel, and interact with (sometimes without even realizing it).

Lighting

Let's start with what we can see. Lighting is a particularly compelling driver of productivity and engagement because it demonstrates such a direct impact on mood. Certain temperatures of light can support mental acuity and wakefulness while other temperatures trigger feelings of friendliness and a desire to share ideas while still others encourage calm and relaxation. The reason for these variations is logical: human beings are designed to engage with the changing light patterns of the sun. In the morning, the light looks different from how it does in the afternoon, at dusk, and at night. It's encoded in our DNA to follow these patterns, and so, when we get into environments with stale, unchanging, often distracting light, our focus, alertness, and even our vitality suffers.

Study after study shows that human beings are simply happier in natural light. In an office setting, providing 100% natural light all the time is impossible, so adopting strategies to harvest and mimic that light is beneficial to the cause of employee engagement. It's often best practice to feature "blue-enriched" lighting in areas where the majority of your staff will be performing their work, as bluer lighting intensifies focus, reduces eye-strain, and lowers melatonin, which helps keep people feeling more alert and awake.

Meeting rooms tend to benefit from warmer lighting, where the stimulation of calm and a sense of trust tends to help close deals.

Conference rooms often see advantages from the middle warmth of lighting, as this combines the alertness effect with the social effect and has been connected to heightened creativity.

There are age and personal preference factors at play too. Depending on your age, you may favor more lighting over the less lighting preferred by younger coworkers. This is why it often helps to offer workspace lighting in addition to the overhead lighting in the main office space. “We’ve found that it’s important to give people choice,” Pete Jefferson said. “This speaks to how we’re wired. We’re inherently more comfortable when we have the ability to control our environments. Whether it’s window shades, dimmable lights, or the ability to shape our own workstation environments, it’s all important to a person’s overall wellbeing.”

When addressing the lighting design for one of their clients, BranchPattern focuses on how the spaces are modeled. “We do daylight modeling and lighting modeling to determine contrast ratios and appropriate levels of light in every space of the office,” Pete said. “The architecture of the building will dictate how to design the artificial lighting, how to lay out the workstations, which directions each monitor should be facing, and so on. All these light sources need to be working in harmony.”

Natural, variable, and adjustable. This is the name of the game in modern lighting. Some companies get by with different light temperatures in different spaces, lights that can be dimmed or brightened accordingly, but others are finding even greater advantage in lighting systems that adjust based on the ambient light streaming in from outside.

I’ve mentioned the term “daylight harvesting” a couple times already, and it is very much the future. We feature this system at the Bentley, and our employees will tell you that it absolutely improves their mood and sense of wellbeing. If human beings are designed to engage with the slowly changing light temperatures of the sun over the course of a day, then being able to mimic those same patterns inside your main office space helps optimize their productivity.

More directly, daylight harvesting automatically ensures that you drastically reduce strain on the eyes. In a traditional working environment, if the light is too dim, you're straining to read. Too bright, and you're squinting for comfort. With better, more natural lighting control, reading becomes easier and more comfortable, which drives up levels of concentration and engagement with the task at hand.

Ergonomics

Ergonomics isn't exactly a new entrant to the game of employee engagement, but the way we think about the subject is changing. The research on the negative health impact of sitting for prolonged periods is extensive and compelling. For this reason, many employers are trending toward standing desks, or ideally, desks that offer the ability to vary between sitting and standing. Not everyone enjoys (or is even comfortable) standing all day, so having the flexibility is a positive. Sit-stand desks are especially beneficial for offices where less space is available.

"But sit/stand isn't a panacea either," Pete Jefferson warned. "They're a tool in the toolbox, but they can't solve all the problems with ergonomics or physical health. We've seen the studies about how sitting all day can be as damaging as smoking two packs a day. But recent studies show that standing for long periods has its own health risks. It makes sense. We weren't designed to sit all day or stand still all day. What's important is movement and variability. This is part of why stimulating people to just get out of their chairs is becoming a trend."

So the ideal ergonomic situation is one where the employee feels comfortable sitting or standing at the main workspace, comfortable in varied chairs or standing spaces in breakout rooms, conference rooms, or other collaborative spaces, comfortable in the café, and comfortable with the prospect of using the fitness center in the middle of the day. Put another way, ideal ergonomics isn't a matter of lessening a person's discomfort in their individual workspace, it's about ensuring variability of comfort over the course of the day and encouraging them to move around.

Thermal Comfort

I can't stress enough how significant a factor thermal comfort is to employee wellbeing and productivity. It is arguably the most important factor to consider at the outset, because so many spaces get it wrong. "The big thing here is that most people just think about air temperature," Pete pointed out. And it's true. The number one tenant complaint for any management company is that it's either too hot or too cold in the building and the temperature needs to be adjusted. I've mentioned already the many different factors at play that make this so, but if you're going to cut down on these complaints and sharpen employee focus, then temperature is really just one component.

The standards used to predict thermal comfort measure six criteria in a given space: air temperature, relative humidity, air velocity, metabolic rate, clothing level, and radiant temperature. "It starts with understanding how human beings work physiologically and then reflecting that in the envelope of the building design," Pete explains. "The quality and proximity of the glass and exterior walls is a major factor. Way too many designers push people up against the glass, where it will be hot in summer and cold in winter, and in response, the engineer will put diffusers right above this person, which will dump hot air or cold air directly on them from the HVAC. For these people, even if the thermostat reads 72 degrees, they're going to be uncomfortable because they're sitting next to hot glass under a curtain of 55-degree air from the A/C."

Then there is also humidity. Keeping the relative humidity levels in your office between 30% and 40% year-round can change nearly everything about the health of your people. A consistent, optimal humidity level prevents dehydration, dry skin, eye discomfort, and nose and throat dryness. These improvements lead to a substantial drop in the rate of laryngitis, influenza, and the common cold. It also reduces the existence and effects of bacteria, viruses, fungi, mites, respiratory infections, allergies, and asthma. If you're concerned about the condition of the materials in the office, optimal humidity also helps prevent damage and prolong the life of paper, leather, wood, books, art, packaging, glue, food, concrete, and on and on. Plus, because it reduces static charge, you can expect better performance from your electronic equipment, less danger around flammables, and greater overall comfort when walking across a carpet or sitting on furniture.[3]

Imagine the boost in productivity and the reduction in costly absenteeism you can expect if all of these things are true. And this is just what better *humidity* can do. Other studies have shown that better ventilation can improve worker productivity by up to 11%, and better lighting can lead to a 23% productivity increase.[4] Offices with a focus on wellness enjoy a 26% improvement in worker cognition, and 30% fewer illness-related absences.[5]

"I would argue that from a cognitive function standpoint, the best evidence is to provide people with more fresh air," Pete said. "There are very strong correlations between ventilation rates and productivity. We do our best work when the CO_2 levels are similar to what you will find outside." This is why so many modern ventilation systems incorporate strategies to pull more air from outside while simultaneously monitoring and regulating thermal comfort in dynamic new ways. You get the best cognitive function when the CO_2 levels inside the office are almost *exactly* like ideal conditions outside.

Acoustics

Now, I am very much an advocate of open office design, but I also recognize one of its major potential weaknesses. I use the word "potential" because there are plenty of strategies for overcoming it. But the trick is that you have to actually pay attention to acoustics during the design process. In 1994, when Blattner Brunner, Inc., made the leap to their first open office, they soon learned that they had made this same common oversight in their planning. We'll need to cut them some slack here, though, because we're talking about 1994, and they were essentially pioneering the open office movement (at least in Pittsburgh). In their first open space, they went with tall panels around workspaces, closed doors for executive offices, high ceilings, and no means to control ambient sound. "You could hear every conversation, every phone ringing, every click of a hard-soled shoe against the floor," Joe Blattner

3 http://www.ahrinet.org/App_Content/ahri/files/Humidity_Occupants_Presentation.pdf
4 Blinch, Russ. "Healthy Buildings: Why Workers Are Demanding Sustainable Offices." The Guardian. May 29, 2014.
5 Gaskell, Adi. "A Green Office Equals a Productive Office." Forbes.com. February 15, 2017.

said. "Because there were no systems in place to attenuate that sound, the main office space would get to where you could hardly hear yourself think."

They learned from this mistake, and in the lead-up to their next move in 1998, they took steps to eliminate it. "We installed an expensive system that would pump out white noise everywhere except in the meeting rooms," Joe said. Where before, staff essentially had to shout over background noise, now the white noise ensured a more comfortable level of sound management. It might seem counterintuitive, the idea of introducing noise to help mitigate noise, but the effects are astonishing.

Thanks to an array of speakers placed every twenty feet into acoustically engineered ceiling tiles, the new office design ensured that the company could deliver white noise at a level so low that it was hardly noticeable. Meanwhile, you could speak and interact with people near you at a normal, comfortable volume even while the undetectable white noise deadened the sound of conversations happening twenty feet away. It removed the clarity of distant conversations in much the same way that a six-foot-high barrier might—all without having to accept the sightline losses associated with six-foot-high barriers.

Curiously, keeping those barriers low has a way of softening the background noise, as well. Sure, you're losing the noise-deadening that a barrier creates naturally. But there's an interesting thing that happens when you can actually *see* your coworkers at all times: you don't speak as loudly. If you take a personal call in a more enclosed environment, you might be inclined to speak louder. But if you can see that there are other people within earshot, you tend to speak at a much lower volume—a volume, incidentally, that imperceptible white noise neutralizes for anyone otherwise within earshot.

The strategies have only had to enhance in the years since 1998, as well—and partly because the sheer number of elements in a modern office that contribute to sound has expanded so considerably. It never ceases to amaze how often businesses will concentrate their efforts on including all the latest and greatest technologies and amenities without considering the *sounds* they make. They install all those bells and whistles without considering the actual noise of the bells and whistles.

Now, in an open or semi-open office setting, you have jolty Skype conversations happening over one shoulder, a remote webinar in front of you, a speakerphone conversation behind you, and a boisterous conversation between a small group in the café to your left, where there's also the ambient hum of the refrigerator or the swooshing of a running dishwasher. Not only does all this make it harder for you to hear yourself think, it also makes it more difficult to communicate. It's tougher to hear and be heard during otherwise productive conversations—and worse yet, many employees in open or semi-open spaces with poor acoustics fight the problem by plugging in some earbuds or giant headphones. This can take the positive investment toward open and shared spaces and *reverse* their impact by way of isolating people from one another.

Whatever the design of the space, the bottom line is that the more time you spend engaging with unpleasant, unexpected, or otherwise invasive sound, the more time you spend distracted and unengaged.

Fitness

I've mentioned already the way the presence of a fitness center can impact culture, individual wellbeing, and productivity. But another matter to consider is that not all employees value the same things in their fitness centers. Here is another area where flexibility is the name of the game. Step one is ensuring that there is a wide range of equipment in the space. Not everyone loves the elliptical, and not everyone wants to hit the weights. The more choices they have, the more they will be satisfied with the amenity. Further, consider offering a range of classes led by different fitness instructors with backgrounds in various disciplines.

Don't forget about the music and lighting, either. Some people prefer their exercise space to be brighter than others, and some people would rather avoid the intensity of heavy metal. The more your people feel like they are empowered to make their exercise space their own, the more often they will use it. The more often they use it, the more productivity your company will gain.

It might seem counterintuitive to ask people to spend less time at their desks and in return receive better productivity, but consider the benefits. Study after study has shown that access to fitness improves job satisfaction, reduces stress, makes employees more motivated and creative, compels them to show up for work more often, and increases productivity to the tune of 12%.[6] Exercise makes people happier, makes their neurotransmitters fire at more engaged rates, and even helps them sleep better. All of this leads to a more engaged, sharper minded, *happier* employee—all of which perpetuates that productivity increase. And as an added benefit, the more your staff exercises, the lower your healthcare costs.

Social Interaction

The final element of keeping your people optimally engaged is offering the opportunity for social interaction. Stress levels decrease when we socialize, and this has a positive impact on engagement, collaboration, and productivity.

Part of stimulating social interaction goes back to Pete Jefferson's point about the value of getting people away from their desks over the course of the day. It's not just an ergonomics thing. Getting people up and moving is also about social interaction, which helps stimulate wellbeing and productivity. If you're compelled to leave your workspace more often and seek out alternate spaces to work, then you're more likely to meet people by accident, share a little cross-talk between company disciplines, collaborate, and make meaningful connections.

In keeping with the theme of flexibility, the more varied the social/ collaborative environments you offer your people, the more likely they are to engage in these accidental meetings and cross-talk. With these factors comes enhanced collaboration and innovation, which improves productivity, and in fact, strengthens cultural cohesion and even employee loyalty. The more of these factors you keep in play—and the more you keep them flexible (and agile for when the market changes or upgrades become necessary)—the more likely your company is to benefit from innovation, knowledge growth, brand enhancement, cultural cohesion, and marked increases in productivity.

---

6 Crawford, Charles. "9 Reasons Why Encouraging Fitness In the Office Is Beneficial." Business.com. February 22, 2017.

COMMUNICATE YOUR CARE

With all the latest data and research pointing to how significantly these environmental stimuli impact overall wellness and productivity, the question is how do you ensure that you're making the right choices relative to these factors when choosing and designing a new space? For BranchPattern, it's a human-centered design model: Discovery, Iteration, Validation, and Evolution (DIVE).

"For *Discovery*, we start by evaluating an organization's existing space performances through the use of research and pre-occupancy evaluations," Pete Jefferson explained. "We find that 60-80% of the people we interview have information about their built environment that they want to share. From there, we use that information to set performance targets. We're looking at things like appropriate energy goals, certification levels for the building, or the desire that the occupants might have for a nature-rich environment."

With *Iteration*, BranchPattern uses computer simulations to model building performance to predict energy consumption, daylighting levels, thermal comfort, and acoustics. "We iterate until we come up with an elegant solution that hits the budget, performance targets, and design considerations."

The *Validation* phase generally includes a lot of testing of the building systems, from mechanical systems to building enclosures, all with an eye toward the indoor environmental quality that they create. "We think about buildings as a system, and the people who occupy it are a part of that system. There's a strong connection between indoor environmental quality and the energy performance of buildings, so we believe that if we can target great IEQ outcomes, we'll also get great energy performance with fewer operational headaches."

Finally, with *Evolution*, BranchPattern performs Post-Occupancy Evaluations (POEs), meaning they make observations of how the people are using and reacting to the space. This includes surveys of the occupants, as well as the maintenance staff, to see whether everyone is meeting the expected levels of maintainability and comfort.

The ultimate goal is to produce what JLL refers to as a "green + productive workplace." "We're seeking a balance between sustainability, wellness, and energy efficiency," said JC Pelusi, International Director, Corporate Solutions and the Great Lakes Region at JLL. "The best environment is one where everyone is comfortable and feels like they're supported physically and mentally. This makes them more productive and more likely to stay with the company."

That final point is really prescient, in that it speaks to how focusing on these factors contributes not just to better, happier, harder work, but also a person's loyalty. We're still trying to cut down on turnover, after all, and one of the best ways to do that is to clearly demonstrate that you are concerned for your people's health and wellbeing. I really can't stress enough how important it is to use your office space as a means to communicate to your people how much you care about them. The quality of the air, light, water, and acoustics can make all the difference on that front, and it *absolutely* helps if you find ways to tell them about what you're doing.

At Burns Scalo, we like the idea of improved health and cognition with fewer absences, so we have already committed to these elements. But again, for the effect to be strongest, you have to go beyond just the monitors and systems necessary to make the space as comfortable as possible. Taking care of your people is an ongoing task and a long-term strategy.

On the cultural side, at Burns Scalo we promote healthy competitions like the stair-climbing challenge in the office, weight loss contests, and back in January, the polar plunge. Whatever it is, we make sure that we run a health and wellness promotion at least once every two months. Of course they don't all appeal to every person on the staff, but most people find interest in at least one promotion over the course of the year. And no matter how many contests each person takes part in, just having them drastically improves our staff cohesion and promotes team building.

In other words, not only does this help keep health and wellness closer to the forefront of everyone's minds, it also helps boost that essential chemistry at the heart of a strong culture and a strong brand. These kinds of initiatives tend to get people to bond more authentically with people who aren't part of their usual working roles. Every time you can get the right colleagues together, and they're feeling healthy and happy as they work on something different and outside the box, it's magic. It's like 1+1+1=5. Those three people, having done something challenging and remarkable and not-work-related together suddenly have the kind of social chemistry that allows them to produce together professionally on a whole new level.

On top of that, people who come into our building see all of this in the way our staff is healthy, happy, and engaged with each other. Our culture is strong, and thanks to our commitment to wellness, so is our brand. As an aside, this also helps tremendously with recruiting, because most people are more eager to join a team like this and work in an environment like this. But it also helps with retention, because if you have good colleagues, friends, and shared experiences in a healthy workplace, it becomes that much more difficult to justify leaving for another employer.

CHAPTER 7

OPEN OFFICE, OPEN MINDS

"Give me the luxuries of life
and I will willingly do without the necessities."
- Frank Lloyd Wright

When I was first starting out in business in the mid-80s, everyone in management or above had a four-walled office with a door they could close. The highest levels occupied the offices with actual windows. The c-suite took the sprawling corner offices. For the frontline employees—everyone from entry-level to support staff to customer-facing staff—they had to cram into high-walled cubicles. Sometimes a person's workspace would be designed in a fashion specific to his/her role with the company, but even in those cases, the specifications weren't all that dissimilar from the workspaces designed for other roles.

Back then, companies in every industry favored uniformity, privacy, rigid formality, and top-down structures that demanded their employees to just keep their heads down and work. That was back before the concept of work/life balance, and long before work-life blend. That was back when people believed that the way you drove productivity was to reward the higher-ups with all the perks while making the lower level employees churn out the work in the hopes that one day they might climb the ladder. That message you wanted to promote to anyone who walked into your lobby was, "This is a place where work happens. *Only* work."

Those days are over. Between the talent war, changing demographics, the growing need to align employee self-interest with company interest, and the awakening to the notion that modern offices don't cost much more money while also *saving* and *making* you money in the long-term, the best and brightest companies in the world are making the switch to more open designs. As we will explore in this chapter, those companies are quickly discovering that open offices lead to more open *minds* among the staff—and open minds tend to positively impact the bottom line.

Photo: Careform – Architectural design by NEXT Architecture, photo by Mike Leonardi.

Despite all this, there is still quite a bit of pushback from decision-makers, brokers, and other industry insiders about the perceived shortcomings of open offices. Part of the problem is that when some people hear “open office design,” they picture the most extreme version of the concept: ultra-minimalist spaces with huge glass walls, no offices or cubicles, and everyone lining up shoulder to shoulder in identical bench seating with no partitions between them. So before we start talking misconceptions about open office, let’s get one thing clear: while that kind of design works for some companies, I’m not advocating for anything so drastic. In our experience, the best companies are moving toward a hybrid version of the traditional office and more modern, open designs. More on this later. First, the misconceptions.

The objections to open offices typically come from three different misconceptions. First, there’s the assumption that open offices are only for the technology industry, and just don’t fit the culture of companies that belong to more buttoned-down industries. Second, there is this notion that if you commit to creating a well-designed and amenity-driven space, you wind up attracting the kind of talent that feels *entitled* to these things. And finally, some seem to think that there is a direct correlation between productivity and access to privacy, and if these open spaces remove some measure of privacy, then it only stands to reason that productivity will suffer as a result.

So, in defense of modern, more open office designs, let’s dispel those misconceptions, one by one.

OPEN OFFICES ARE FOR EVERYONE

I cut my teeth as a professional in a private office setting, so I completely understand the assumption that open office design is nothing more than a fad. Private spaces worked so well for people of my generation for such a long time; why should it be any different today? We’ve already discussed how *completely* different the work styles are for younger generations, and how the advance of technology has changed the way we think about the work-life blend, so I won’t jump back into that argument. What matters is that the trend toward open office is happening across *every* industry (not just technology, and not just with Fortune 500 companies, either), and given the preferences of younger generations, that trend isn't changing anytime soon.

To get to the heart of why, I posed the question to a couple industry insiders from CBRE, the world's largest commercial real estate services and investment firm. According to Patrick Gruden, First Vice President with the Corporate Advisory Services Group of CBRE's Pittsburgh office, open offices are absolutely *not* just for the technology industry. In fact, the trend in every industry is toward higher quality office space that focuses on health and wellness—and increasingly, those spaces are a hybrid of open and private office designs. "It's driven mostly by Millennials," Patrick explained, "but talent in general is demanding higher quality buildings, more amenities, and more open and flexible workspaces."

David Koch, Executive Vice President of the Corporate Advisory Services Group of CBRE's Pittsburgh office, agrees that while Millennials are driving the change, the desire for more open, collaborative space extends to every generation. "The older generations are realizing that the perimeter offices with interior workstations are going the way of the typewriter," he said. This movement starts with the notion that it's easier to attract and retain highly talented employees when you can trumpet great amenities, social opportunities, and a focus on wellness. But where the RPMs really start to fire is when you get into the way open, amenitized offices enhance productivity, as well. "Most companies we deal with are interested in natural light, working more collaboratively, and having amenities within a close proximity to their location. 'Live, work, play' has become the mantra for companies [of every industry]."

The question, though, is how much longer will this mantra stick around? What will office designs look like five to ten years from now? "You'll see more smart-office environments," Patrick said. "More open, creative, and flexible work environments with lots of employee amenities all focused on productive environments, recruitment, and retention." David, meanwhile, believed that, "more and more companies will embrace allowing employees to share space and work in the more urban areas where it all began. What goes around comes around."

YOUR SPACE IS YOUR CULTURE

The reason that industry insiders like Patrick and David can be so certain of the staying power of these trends is that demographic shift. If you want to attract the best talent, you have to give that talent what it wants. And what the talent wants is to work in a space that reflects a culture they can believe in. Every great business implements strategies to build a positive and productive culture. But no matter how many times you reiterate your mission and purpose, you don't get all the way there without a space that both complements and drives that culture. The space is the supplemental tool that sets the pace.

Of course staff occupies the space most often, but don't overlook the added benefits to be found in the way the client or prospect perceives the company. "Our desire was to hire the best and the brightest," Joe Blattner said. "But our objective was to be the most desired agency to work for or with—the kind that lands the most sought-after clients." When Blattner Brunner, Inc. upgraded to their first open office space in downtown Pittsburgh, one of the primary focuses of the design was around the idea that they had to show well during the agency tour. When a client came in, they wanted to be able to use their physical space as a projection of their culture, which would in turn provide leverage in the intense battle for a prospect's business.

If you can walk a prospect through the space, and there are all these open sightlines and creative areas, and you see everyone working and collaborating and meeting, and you feel all that *energy*, it's a much more powerful presentation than leading someone from office to office and introducing them to staff. "We had twenty-four integrated practices," Blattner said. "That was unique in our industry. And we could demonstrate that advantage really powerfully through the layout of the space. It was clear that our culture was to have everything integrated, and that everyone worked openly and together. No other firm could replicate that effect simply because they didn't have an open plan."

They extended this message about the best-in-class experience to the services they provided both to staff and to visiting prospects and clients. When you entered the space, you were greeted not by a receptionist, but by a concierge. The concierge would be preparing some artisanal popcorn or a fresh salad and inviting you to try it. The first question would be if there was anything you needed.

If you needed your shoes shined, the concierge would have it taken care of during your meeting. If you needed a cab waiting for you, it would be there. If you had a special lunch order, it would be delivered and set up at the designated time and in the designated food delivery stations outside the conference room in which you were meeting. Whatever you needed, the concierge service would go above and beyond—and this move happened long enough ago that it predated the ubiquitous Internet—to get those needs met. The goal was to project a sense of hospitality and luxury that one simply didn't find anywhere else in the industry.

As a result of the design and of innovations like these, Blattner Brunner began landing all the key accounts they wanted, and were turning away only the work they *didn't* want. "For a long time, we just couldn't miss," Blattner said. The market began talking up the firm because of its work product, but also because of its space. Publications sought opportunities to photograph and profile the offices. This raised their profile to where landing new accounts became even easier, they were able to recruit better and better employees, and productivity climbed higher. "Your office space can be one of the greatest strategic weapons to recruit and retain, but it's also a great way to help sell a best-in-class working culture."

To create a best-in-class working culture, you have to keep in mind that everything matters. If you build a great space and then put terrible furniture in it, you haven't achieved the end you seek. At Burns Scalo, we take every opportunity to connect our employees to the culture, both in the physical space and in terms of our management practices. Everyone's workspaces are designed for their preferences and for their specific roles with the company. We give everybody an iPhone—not just a work phone, but one they can keep for their personal use. On top of that, we pay their personal phone and data plans completely.

This might sound like a relatively small perk, but it goes a long way toward communicating our culture while also engendering positive vibes from the staff. With that free phone and plan—all those free calls, emails, searches, and data—they don't have to think about that bill or when they're going to upgrade their phone because it's all baked right in to their connection with the company. And this is just a *phone*. If you give your staff opportunity and reason to connect personally with every element of their workspaces, those same positive vibes extend to everything they do for you as an employee. It keeps their campfire burning.

We have an online company store full of genuinely great clothing bearing our logo, and we give everyone in the company a stipend to spend at the site. Like those old office designs with uniform workspaces, we used to give everyone the same t-shirt in an effort to create a sense of comradery and uniformity while also advertising our brand. But what do you do with a company t-shirt? You throw it in the bottom of the drawer.

Our stipend strategy, meanwhile, empowers people to purchase whatever they want, which allows them to express their individual identity while also connecting themselves to the culture as a whole. As an added bonus, people are far more likely to actually want to *wear* your company clothing if they have a choice in what they purchase. It helps that this stuff is actually fashionable, but choice does matter—and so does the idea that your employer is willing to buy you a bunch of nice clothes.

Similarly, our employees never have to worry about paying for coffee or snacks. They can meet their need to connect to the outdoors by taking advantage of our patio space and walking trail. They don't need to pay for a gym membership, because they have the fitness center in the building. Their computers are all high-end, cutting edge laptops that they are welcome to take home with them. We provide Uber credits that they can use to get home from work events that serve alcohol. We offer to pick up the tab for annual physicals, life insurance and personal benefits, and we even bring in massage therapists for a complimentary annual massage. We promote healthy practices with weight loss challenges, stairs challenges, and "Walking Wednesdays." We even pay to have our employees' tax returns done for them.

These are all concierge-style amenities, yes, but they are so much more than that. They are a clear and regular reminder of what we stand for as a company. They support our culture—and in a unique way because they are always there (and if you do it right, they're always flexible and agile enough to make room for upgrades). They contribute to stronger chemistry between coworkers because they invite people to share common and collaborative settings. This leads to the free flow of ideas, which drives innovation, which drives profitability. But it all starts with using your space, your amenities, and your practices to show them that you care and want to provide for their needs. If you make them happy first, guess what happens? They return the favor with harder, better, more innovative work.

AMENITIES ARE *NOT* ENTITLEMENTS

I recently had the occasion to attend a fundraising event for a local charity. They threw the event in a flashy new hotel with beautiful architecture, lots of impressive glass, and high-end amenities. Yes, the food and drinks were spectacular, the music was great, and everyone seemed to have a good time. But what made the most profound impression was the message that this extraordinary party sent about the organization that was throwing it. They had a thousand choices to make about how, and just as importantly, *where* to host this fundraiser, but the most important was the decision to throw the party in a memorable space that made everyone say, "Wow!" I gave more to the organization because of that impression, and I know I wasn't alone.

Now, imagine if your office could have this same effect on everyone who ever set foot in it—not just your people, but your clients and partners, as well. Imagine being able to throw a party that gives people a similar impression of luxury and class, and you can throw this party any time you want. How would that affect your client outreach? How would it impact your partnerships? How would your sales improve?

Put simply, exceptional office space is a luxury you must be willing to afford. Amenities are *not* entitlements; they are an exciting new means to drive profit. This is partly because people are more productive when they're comfortable and feel like they've had all their needs met. But in the short term, just like with the Internet of fifteen years ago, amenities drive profits because they are still largely underserved. At the time of this writing, amenities remain a competitive advantage. This won't last long, though. Given the rate that companies are jumping on the bandwagon, soon they will be as common as the Internet, and those who fail to embrace them will be left behind.

So how do we get to where we need to be? What does the appropriate design look like? We'll get a little deeper into the specific steps for finding or designing your ideal space in a moment, but for now, let it be known that the first step is to stop thinking in terms of cost per square foot and start thinking about how you can use your space to serve your staff.

Put another way, stop thinking about how to pinch pennies like a Motel 6 and start thinking like a luxury hotel. High-quality amenities are a great place to start, but concierge services are an excellent way to take the effort to the next level. Every decision you make should come from a place that minimizes concern for the bottom line cost and maximizes concern for your people's technological needs, health, wellbeing, and work-life blend. Design or choose spaces that accentuate what it is that makes you passionate about the company. Move yourself into a space that you and everyone who works for you can be proud of. Do this and that pride will pay for the cost of the new space many times over.

THE EVOLUTION OF OPEN OFFICE

Stale cubicle farms and private offices are going the way of the dinosaur. So too are the starkly open, bench-seating designs. In their place, the industry is lately seeing a refreshing hybrid of open design and private space. These days, the name of the game is finding ways to ensure that every employee, no matter what their generation or their personal preferences, can find a comfortable, productive place to work (and ideally, more than one or two such places). It's all about flexibility in space, a focus on wellness, and an effort to cater to employee satisfaction. There are many ways to approach these needs—and the plan should be unique to the company's culture—but the best designs feature a combination of open, collaborative space and more private, quiet spaces that can accommodate those who need to spend a few hours churning out uninterrupted work.

Dan Delisio, principal and owner of NEXT Architecture, and Chris Pless, principal at NEXT Architecture, have seen this evolution firsthand. "In the early days of open office designs," Chris explained, "it was still very hierarchical. You had the administrative staff out front and the big executives in the back in four-walled offices. Yes, many of the workspaces were more open, but specific to the role was what you got square-footage-wise. But today, it's more about the multigenerational workforces and how you cater to them equally. So the end product is even more open and amenity-driven."

"At the same time," Dan added, "you have to make space for privacy and head-down work that is separate from the open workspaces." The interesting thing about this new design is that if you think back to the way offices used to look when I was first starting my career, everything has essentially flipped.

"The best space used to go to the CEO. Now that space is all collaborative areas. Those spaces that used to go to giant corner offices are now going toward cafés or cafeterias. For most companies it makes sense not just culturally, but in terms of use of space. Those huge CEO offices used to be almost total wastes of space because most CEOs aren't in the office most of the time."

Where before, space and luxury were a sign of where you stood in the hierarchy of the company, now it is a sign of how much (or how little) leadership values the employees that produce the majority of the work.

"The thinking used to be, 'Who cares about the worker?' Now, making the worker comfortable and happy is what it's all about."

If you're going to make dozens, hundreds, or even thousands of different employees (with their own unique and varied tastes and work styles) comfortable and happy, then the best strategy is to create spaces that are as flexible and easy to change as possible. Ideally, you want it to be really simple for every employee to get up from their dedicated workspace and take everything they need to another, equally comfortable, equally connected environment.

DELTA POINT: THE LUXURY SUITE APPROACH

Before we move on to the structure and benefits of open and hybrid-open office designs, there's another common objection we should address head-on: these spaces are too expensive, or aren't efficient enough in terms of cost per square foot. The objection goes that you have to dedicate all this space to common areas that people may or may not use for work. Wouldn't it be better and more cost efficient to just use that space to cram in as many desks as possible?

There might have been a time when this was true—when making room for collaborative spaces meant sacrificing room for workspaces—but those days are very much over. The best and brightest companies we work with at Burns Scalo use every inch of collaborative space in creative ways that increase the value of every square foot. Where before, a lobby was a place exclusively to wait or lounge, the basements were for storage, the hallways were for walking from point A to point B, there were whole rooms dedicated exclusively to the printer, and the rooftops were for nothing more than catching rainwater, modern designs incorporate *all* available space into the effort to create inviting, varied, and productive places to work, meet, and play.

These spaces are far less specialized than they used to be, and far more adaptable. Now you're looking at lobbies with café tables and sofas and all the technology you could need to get your work done just as efficiently as you can at your desk. The same goes for the new rooftop deck, or the new movie/conference projector in the basement lounge. Now you're enjoying that grab and go snack station and the latte machine next to the printer, and the ping-pong table in the hallway.

The central goal is to make every common area into a place where *every* employee in the company will want to be—places that don't just feel like common areas, but like *luxury suites* where the employee, prospect, or client can feel like they are having a host of their needs met in a positive, memorable way. In this way, you aren't simply dedicating space to common areas, but rather, maximizing the use and productivity happening even in the spaces that used to serve only one ancillary purpose.

Not only does this improve the return on investment in your space, but it serves as excellent opportunity to bring your staff together. These kinds of spaces make for perfect venues to host activities that drive collaboration and comradery. Think fitness classes in the fitness center, movie screenings in the basement theater, happy hours in the lounge, and so on. These efforts make your people work better together, they maximize your return on the space, and just as importantly, they keep your people with you longer.

When asked about how to assess the value of an open space design, David Koch of CBRE explained that the cost per square foot is still a good metric, "However, the economic driver now should be the cost of retention of employees. The money, time, and effort can be lost if the employee is unhappy with the building/facility that they work in, and this is far greater than the price per square foot."

At the same time, privacy still matters. There are still times when you need to work privately or communicate on a private matter. There are still client confidentiality issues, proprietary issues, and good old-fashioned home-life matters to consider during traditional working hours, after all. Often, companies that design open office spaces that neglect this occasional need for privacy wind up seeing a drain on overall staff productivity. When a confidential matter arises, employees that work in strictly open environments will lose more productivity time in the act of seeking out a private space. Similarly, those employees who would prefer the opportunity to work in a private space from time to time tend to resent employers who don't provide them that opportunity. Sometimes, collaboration and engagement work best when we're given the opportunity to avoid it when we need to.

The best designs offer spaces of different styles and purposes. The individual desks/workspaces can be open, sure, but it also helps to have collaboration or conference rooms, or even hotel-style private offices where an employee can retreat to a quieter, closed-off environment when the situation calls for it. Further, leadership can designate certain quiet areas, where conversation or phone use is prohibited, while also dedicating areas like the lounge or café for conversation and collaboration. Ideally, every employee should feel invited to use the collaborative spaces at any time, but also, every employee's main workspace should reside within a short walk to a space where they can enjoy some privacy when the need arises.

As Chris and Dan from NEXT Architecture point out, the key to arriving at the best design for your office space is to invite input from the broadest cross-section of your people as possible. "We had a client recently who was designing a new space after one company acquired another," Dan said. "Their goal was to create a design that would help bring the two different cultures together. The acquiring company was used to bigger, more enclosed offices while the other company preferred more open spaces. Our initial process was to sit with a core team and get their thoughts so we could structure our programming around their preferences.

"Next, we staged these constructive workshops where we brought a cross-section of employees together and went through a bunch of images of workspaces for them to rate in terms of preferences. Once we compiled the information, we saw the bigger picture of what the company was looking for."

"It's interesting how the designs can wind up looking different from what the core team was expecting, too," Chris added. "This client started with wanting a lot of glass and a more open concept, but when we showed them the results of the employee surveys, they were like, 'Well, maybe we don't want it quite *that* open." Of course in these cases, it's back to the drawing board. The goal is to use as much input as possible to arrive at deeper observations of how the company and its many employees work. "We try to walk them through a typical day to figure out how to make the company as efficient as possible. It's usually a fun, eye-opening process for the client. The more time you take in that survey phase, the better you'll understand what you're looking for."

"It used to be that executives just made decisions based on cost or even just gut feelings," Dan said. "But the modern design process moves you toward bigger, better data from larger numbers of contributors to the company. This way, if there's something about the design that isn't resonating with someone, you can always go back and answer the questions about *why* you made a given decision. That's an important factor, because it means you're not just grasping at straws."

COLLABORATION, CREATIVITY, COMMITMENT

For those who object to the idea of open office or hybrid office designs, consider that the benefits extend well beyond just greater opportunity to collaborate. The productivity potential of your people winds up improving thanks to two other key factors, as well. Opportunities to meet and be creative together do more than just drive innovation. They also breed commitment to the company.

Think about it this way: if you make a creative contribution to a project, you're more likely to value the success of that project. Creativity makes you more invested in seeing whether your great idea leads to positive results. This isn't just a matter of satisfaction on the work- and project-level either. 33% of employees are more loyal to the companies that allow them opportunities for creative collaboration.[1] Opportunities for creativity have also been directly linked to an employee's sense of wellbeing.

If you want people to be creative, it helps to get them together. Groups are more innovative than individuals. And yes, companies have been following the logic of team-driven project management for years, but true creativity tends to happen literally outside the box. Cram people into a conference room for a brainstorming session, and you might just come up with some creative ideas. But the best ideas are often spur-of-the-moment, discovered when your guard is down and you weren't tasked with thinking about something directly. It's the shower-power effect. People tend to have some of their most creative thoughts in the shower because that's the one time of day when we're allowed to de-stress and not think about anything in particular for a while.

This same effect can happen in many different spaces in a great office, as well. Employees from different backgrounds and teams meeting by accident in the café, the rooftop deck, a breakout space, the gaming space, and on and on—when they meet in settings where a problem at hand *isn't* on the forefront of their mind, they're much better equipped to find a creative solution. Further, these kinds of spaces lead to people sharing ideas across disciplines that wouldn't typically share ideas directly. This can generate remarkably innovative new strategies.

Next, for people to be creative, they need to feel empowered by the idea that they are *invited* to be creative. Put people in an actual box of an office and they won't think outside it. Give them space, the chance to move, and inspiring, engaging surroundings and you don't just *tell* them that their creativity is valued, you *show* them. Further, the space gives them all the tools they need to innovate and find new solutions. Opening up the sightlines from the workspace to other key areas of the office tends to get people thinking beyond their own tasks and more about the company as a whole. Further, those sightlines better connect people to that sense of purpose and social wellbeing simply because they can *see* their coworkers. This invites interaction, communication, collaboration, and from time to time, brilliant ideas.

---

1 Various Authors. "Green + Productive Workplace." JLL.

You can achieve buy-in to creativity and the broader company message by celebrating your people's creative contributions in the physical space itself, as well. Imagine a wall full of pictures, quotes, and stories about the individual and meaningful contributions of every employee whose workspace resides in that room. Each department can have its own wall, or there could be a single wall celebrating the greatest contributions company-wide. Whatever the case, the wall should feature a creative and eye-catching presentation of the ways people have contributed creativity, and stories about the impact that creativity has had on the company. However it is designed, the purpose is to use this physical space to tell the story of what your company stands for, and how it celebrates creativity.

As an aside, there are many management practices that promote creativity, but we've found at Burns Scalo that there's nothing quite like a financial incentive. We require our staff to submit twelve ideas per year. We promote this need and mention it often in our company-wide messaging. In other words, we directly solicit input on how we can do what we do better. Then, in return, if a great idea saves the company money, the contributor of that idea receives 10% of the annual savings in the form of a bonus.

People need a path—a funnel into which to pour their creativity. So while your open space is inviting new ideas, it is also a great practice to provide a physical space for those ideas to take on life. For example, consider breakout spaces lined with "farms" of whiteboards assembled in rows. Great ideas that remain in a single person's head (or even exchanged in a person-to-person email) could die on the vine. But any great ideas that wind up in physical space like on a communal whiteboard suddenly become ideas that can actually be pursued. Further, having a physical space designed to accept ideas helps reinforce that second notion about empowerment. The more people see their coworkers contributing their ideas to the process and into the physical space, the more empowered they feel to share their own ideas.

Achieving a more creative atmosphere is obviously beneficial to the bottom line. Brilliant ideas lead to competitive new strategies and products, which boosts profits. But the often-overlooked benefit to creativity is that it connects employees to their leaders, to the culture, and to the company's purpose. It takes a group of people who might otherwise just feel like a collection of coworkers and binds them together with compelling stories about why they do what they do, and how they're changing the way they do it for the better. It elevates the company beyond a seller of products or services and into a brand with a meaning behind what it does.

POSITIVE PRESSURE

And as one final (and rather enormous) benefit, open and collaborative spaces also drive hard work. You know that old adage about the carrot versus the stick? I can tell you that the stick never works as effectively as the carrot, but more importantly, that compulsion to work is highest when it's driven not by the leadership, but by an employee's coworkers. Think about it this way: if I'm in a walled-off office, the only thing I can see is the work in front of me. This might seem like a good thing, if you're of the mind that the only way to get work done is to self-motivate, but consider all that positive peer pressure you're sacrificing by settling in behind those walls.

Yes, people drive each other to work harder and better. This is because the people around us tend to shape our day to day habits. These days, with constant social media access and a more authentic connection to people, ideas, and news from all around the world (24/7), people absorb that outside energy more than ever before. This is why an employee's performance can depend heavily on what they *see* happening all around them. If all they see is walls, then all they know is what *they* are doing. But if there are no sightline or sound barriers between where they work and where other people work? The positive traits of other workers tend to translate to them, and vice versa.

At Blattner Brunner, Inc., leaving the walls low served as a visual reinforcement that when you see someone at the desk across from you working hard, you're thinking, "Why am I just sitting here playing Solitaire?" Further, low walls meant that the staff could add a personal touch with art and toys and other expressions of their identities on display for all to see. "Low walls help bring the fun and creativity back into the environment," Blattner explained.

On top of that, Lynne Schultz from Waldron Private Wealth describes her recent move to the more open spaces at the Beacon like this: "At my old job, my office was more private, so I could just pile up all these files of work that I had to get to. It was kind of overwhelming to look at. But the openness of the space at Waldron forces you to be more organized, so you're not bogged down by all the work piled up on your desk. Socially, you're constantly hearing other conversations, which forces you to collaborate and step up your game because you know that your coworkers are getting things done. That's the way it should be. The space and your opportunities to collaborate should push you and all your coworkers toward better work."

Those last two words, "Better Work," carry a double meaning in this case. The first is the more obvious: open up sightlines, offer collaborative space as well as private space, and invite opportunity for collaboration and creativity, and your people will *do* better work. But at the same time, if they can always *see* and *interact* with the people around them, then they're going to see all that work getting done, which is going to compel them to think, "I'd better get to work too." In this way, through greater opportunity for creativity, collaboration, and commitment, and with a healthy dose of positive peer pressure, your open space becomes so much more than just an office; it becomes a place where *better* work gets done.

PART 3:
MONEY

CHAPTER 8

FLIP THE VALUE PROPOSITION

"The memory of bad quality
lasts longer than the shock of high prices."
- Quote from a Fortune Cookie

Recently I had lunch with a friend who had just bought a new house. He and his wife had gone into the search knowing exactly what they wanted, so they'd assumed that they would quickly find the right place for their family. They were wrong. The process wound up being long and exhausting.

"There were just so many factors that meant more to us than we thought they would," my friend explained. There were the obvious things like the number of bedrooms; the quality of the kitchen and bathrooms; the condition of the driveway, the roof, the windows, and the climate control; the size of the yard; and the number of luxury amenities. And then there were the other factors that limited their search in ways they hadn't anticipated: the proximity to work; the commute times; the tax rate; and the quality of the neighborhood, the school system, and the local government.

"When we started the process," he said, "I had a number in mind for what I wanted to pay for the mortgage." That number helped him narrow the search, but in the end, the total mortgage payment wasn't anywhere near the top reason he and his wife made their final choice. Ultimately, they decided that they were willing to pay more than their original projection, because really, what's a couple hundred extra dollars a month if it's the difference between living in a house you kind of like and living in your dream home? "We figured we're going to spend a huge part of our lives in this house," my friend said, "so why not make it a place where we're comfortable and happy with everything?"

Most people who have ever set out to buy a new house can identify with my friend's story. And I'd wager that most people do exactly what he

---

Photo: Frost Todd Brown – Architectural design by NEXT Architecture, photo by Mike Leonardi.

did. It's just so easy to justify going over cost when you're talking about the quality of the place where you and your family will spend most of your time each day. We don't usually think about our office space in the same light, even though many of us spend more of our waking weekday hours at the office than we do at home. I've been involved in hundreds of these transactions, and it never ceases to amaze me how almost everyone asks the same question first:

"What's the rent?"

It never fails. When considering the home they will buy, almost no one places the mortgage payment at the top of their list of deciding factors. But when mulling one of the most important decisions they will ever make for their employees' quality of work life, and for their company's ultimate productivity, most people primarily think about what it's going to cost them (even if it's only going to cost them an almost *incidental* 3% to 7% of their total operating budget). As a result, everyone from agents to brokers to consultants to occupiers frame the commercial office space value proposition pretty much completely upside down. Here is the order that most people rank the top ten items on a traditional value proposition:

1. Rent (or price)
2. Total space
3. Track record of the landlord
4. Location
5. Age of building
6. Mechanical systems
7. Technology
8. Amenities
9. Wellness and Sustainability
10. Employee recruitment/retention

Now, some of those factors are pretty well-placed. Obviously, space is a key component, and as we saw in chapter 4, location is as important today as it has ever been (even if the way we think about location has to change if we're going to stay competitive for talent). Nobody wants a bad landlord. And the age of the building, the quality of the mechanical systems, and the available technology are all significant factors, as well. The bottom three we can rank in just about any order according to a company's identity and culture. But here's the thing: those three at the bottom are increasingly important to business success. And here's the other thing: anyone who allows rent or price to drive this value proposition is going to get left behind.

A huge part of the reason my friend was willing to pay more for the mortgage than originally planned was because of his kids. He and his wife wanted them to be proud of their home, and to be as comfortable and happy there as possible. That didn't mean negotiating and settling for the best mortgage they could get. The kids would never even know what the mortgage was in the first place, and even if they did know, they wouldn't care. What mattered more than the mortgage was nearly every other item on that value proposition list.

Now, the employees of your company aren't your children, but they probably care just exactly as much about your rent as your kids do about your mortgage. They aren't ever going to see your rent bill. All they will see is the quality of the building you put them in. So, why allow rent to be such a key (and often *leading*) determining factor?

To make a strong choice in where to house your company, the first things you should worry about are all those elements that will a) help you attract top talent, b) help you keep the talent you already have, and c) ensure the highest possible quality of work-life and productivity from a happier, healthier, more engaged, and more *present* staff. Don't make your choice based first on the rent bill; make it based on how your people will respond to the space you choose for them. Yes, business is about making money, and the rent bill plays a factor in that equation, but if it's the difference between improving the bottom line and doing the right thing for your people, why not do both?

DELTA POINT:
SMALL ADJUSTMENTS CAN MAKE THE GREATEST IMPACT

Whenever I think about how turning the traditional value proposition upside down can impact employee productivity, I think about Rice Energy. When the search team at Rice Energy called my team in to work with Jamie Rogers on the design of the building, our first task was to determine how we could use the company's identity to shape their new office space. "We owed part of our success to challenging the status quo in our industry," Jamie said. "So we wanted to do the same thing with the building."

From a design perspective, the building turned out to be spectacular, but unpretentious. At 150,000 square feet of total space, it dedicated a full 15,000 of those square feet on the first floor to a state of the art fitness center and a healthy, regionally-sourced cafeteria run by an executive chef. Each floor was designed with collaborative spaces in mind, with only sixty to seventy private offices. And wherever they could, Rogers and the rest of the search team looked to leverage relatively minor expenses toward better health and wellbeing for their employees.

That one-time expense in the fitness center ensured an endless benefit for everyone who put it to good use, as it encouraged healthy behavior and stimulated productivity through physical activity. And the choice to have the company subsidize the cost of the food in the cafeteria allowed for anyone to get a sandwich for a mere $3, or even an extraordinary meal to take home to their families (and at a price far less than they ever could at a local restaurant).

Until you dig deeper, this might sound like a big expense for a small return, but the truth is that the smartest employers recognize that any time an employee feels compelled to get in the car (whether it's to get lunch or drive to where they can get some exercise or run an errand), you lose more than an hour of productivity. With the commute to another location, the transition to and from the car, the time it takes for a decent meal/workout/errand, and then the return transition and trip, it's really, really difficult to get back in even just an hour. Plus, once you've broken your more productive routine, it takes additional time just to get yourself focused and back in the game.

"When you look at the cost of these amenities on a per-employee basis," Jamie said, "we're talking about a nominal amount of money compared to the returns we're seeing with productivity. People translate the quality of their space to the quality of their work. We gave them a respectable work area, and the productivity has improved across the board. Most people eat as a team now. They exercise together. The building and its amenities make everyone's lives easier. And that has also helped our image tremendously."

Jamie estimates that, in addition to the first floor, 10% of the building is dedicated to collaborative space. They could have easily made the choice to pack that space with cubicles and hire as many people as possible in response to the high rate of turnover in their competitive industry. But instead, they dedicated that space to enhancing the employee experience under the assumption that recruiting and retention would improve right along with productivity.

They were right. The building has been an extraordinary recruiting tool—just another way that this David of a company stands up to the many Goliaths in the industry in the war for top talent. "Our industry is hypercompetitive on benefits, cash bonuses, and salaries," Rogers said. "So the building is a big differentiator for us. Nobody else offers the same level of building-related perks as we do." The results speak for themselves. In a job market where companies strive to keep their attrition rate around 5%, Rice Energy's has dropped to below 2%.

"We wound up in a much better place than we would have if we'd led with our bias toward cost-savings," Rogers added. "But at this point, nobody at any level is complaining about it costing too much."

A BRAND-NEW PROPOSITION

These changes in how people work and how they live have a clear impact on the traditional value proposition. We don't necessarily need to invert the list precisely, but we can certainly flip it (almost) on its head. The new value proposition should look something like this:

1. Location
2. Total space
3. Technology
4. Employee recruitment/retention
5. Amenities
6. Wellness and Sustainability
7. Mechanical systems
8. Track record of the landlord
9. Age of building
10. Rent (or price)

The first thing you'll note is that location and space maintain their positions near the top of the list. But as we've seen already, the way we assess them is drastically different, and the data we can use to make quality choices is far enhanced, thanks to recent advances in technology. Like anything else in modern business, it's all about efficiency. New data-collection capabilities allow the design of more efficient layouts for contemporary office environments, including adaptable furniture systems that maximize use of space. The effort streamlines the space dedicated to common areas and can help reduce overall space requirements by 10% to 20%. This is part of why considering rent or cost first is so problematic. Why worry so much about rent when: 1) at 3% to 7%, it's such an insignificant portion of your total operating budget, 2) the cost difference in renting an outdated space and a premium space is so small, and 3) modern design can save you up to 20% of the total space you need.

Of course technology remains near the top of the list, and its impact will only increase between now and 2030, as connectivity grows ever stronger, automation continues changing the way businesses operate, digital mobility becomes more ubiquitous, and companies begin integrating Artificial Intelligence into the daily workflow. In many ways, we are facing cultural and technological pressures that impact the way we work on a level not seen since the Industrial Revolution. In this data-driven, digital age full of rapid, almost overnight change, only the most agile and adaptable companies will survive and thrive. Keeping that agility and adaptability in mind when choosing and designing an office space is paramount.

Employee recruitment and retention comes next because, as we've discussed, the talent war will only intensify in the years to come. Most employers expend considerable resources to attract, train, and retain employees. A well-designed office space reflects not only the company's image and work ethic, but is a crucial component of successful hiring practices, stable employee tenure, and long-term retention of any company's or organization's most valuable assets: its people.

Complicating the talent war is the skills gap, which is widening with every passing year. "The National Federation of Independent Business reports that 45% of small businesses were unable to find qualified candidates to fill job openings and 60% of all employers have job openings that stay vacant for twelve weeks or longer, which costs them $800,000 annually in lost productivity and advertising fees."[1] With the constant flow of technological advancement, and the encroachment of automation on the jobs picture, roles change and then become obsolete at far more rapid rates than ever before. Companies that can use their office space to help attract and retain more talented people will find themselves better equipped to train upward for these ever-changing and ever-more-demanding roles. Along the way, those with the best amenities will be in better position to reduce costly absenteeism and turnover.

Next up is amenities, as they are one of the most direct means to attracting and retaining talent, and also improving the employee's quality of work-life blend, and as a result, their productivity. The key here is to consider the *vibe* of both internal and external amenities. Just because we're talking about space efficiency and multi-use common areas, that doesn't mean spartan design features and layout compromises.

1 "10 Workplace Trends You'll See in 2018." Dan Schawbel. Forbes. November, 2017. https://www.forbes.com/sites/danschawbel/2017/11/01/10-workplace-trends-youll-see-in-2018/#4fc203b4bf22

Modern office space design can often allocate for collaborative meeting areas, open cafés, multiple sizes of conference rooms, inviting reception areas, and fitness areas with the open plan and natural light contributing to a far more productive work environment. The size of the project or investment usually dictates the extent that owners of all new buildings or full-scale renovations of existing properties recognize the importance for common area amenities and strongly consider additional amenities (such as integrated classroom-style or auditorium conferencing with high-tech connectivity, ground-floor restaurants or coffee shops, external patios, and rooftop decks).

For most, seeing "Wellness and Sustainability" so high on the list might seem startling, but it's important to keep in mind that 1) people prefer to work for companies that have their wellness in mind, as well as the impact they're making on the environment and the world at large, and 2) the customer cares about these things, too, and often lets you know with their wallets.

To the first point, incorporating eco-friendly and sustainable building and management practices is simply the right thing to do, but by implementing these practices, landlords and tenants both win. Landlords can certainly promote their conscientious efforts while employers realize that "eco-friendly" and "sustainability" are heavily embedded into the vocabulary of Millennials. While impacts of daylight harvesting, lighting controls, air quality, LED lighting, and Low-E glass are evident, low VOC's (Volatile Organic Compounds), solar energy, water collection, managed recycling, and more are also not only becoming corporate mandates, but highly noticeable aspects for coveted employees considering places of employment.

On the second point, more than ever before, consumers place their trust in companies that do the right thing for their employees, and for the people they impact. Stories abound in social media about how the employee experience can translate into either a positive or negative response from a consumer base. If you treat your people well, and you demonstrate a conscious effort to lower your impact on the environment, the public will know about it, and the return will be measurable.

Mechanical systems come next because no one wants to pay more than they have to for optimal building performance. Technology plays a major role in the way we think about mechanical systems these days, as well. The Internet of Things allows us to track power, light, and temperature fluctuations and usage. Having this data in turn makes it possible to adjust and optimize these elements in ways never before seen. These systems allow new buildings to outperform their aging counterparts. They also save on operating cost, improve operational efficiency, and help track and predict when maintenance will be necessary. More importantly, with modern mechanical systems, your people enjoy better overall comfort levels, which directly translates into lower absenteeism and turnover and higher productivity.

We close with the triumvirate of factors that far too many decision makers still place at or near the top of their value propositions. No one wants a bad landlord, of course, so if all other elements are equal, that begins to factor into the decision. The same goes with the age of the building. Old buildings don't tend to perform as well as newer ones, but with the right systems and the right planning, age can be rendered a far less important factor. Finally, there is the rent.

"There will always be a certain subset of the occupier population that is going to have rental rates as their highest priority," said Dan Adamski, Managing Director of the Pittsburgh office of JLL. "But there's a trend that more and more companies are looking at more holistic measures instead of thinking just about cost per square foot. They're using real estate as not just an expense, but as a means to improve productivity, and as an offensive weapon in that war for talent.

"Anecdotally, we once worked with a company that opened a big office in Pittsburgh with the plan to hire five hundred employees. Their head of real estate told us his goal was to get the cheapest space possible. We got that for them, and they were happy about the deal. But then, two years later, they had to close the office because they couldn't *hire* anybody. They're the perfect example of what can happen when you get a great real estate deal, but a poor operations deal."

Of course none of this is to say that higher rent always equals a better decision. Rather, instead of leading with the question about the rent, we should be leading with the efficiency of space, mechanical systems, and the dramatic and measurable increase in employee productivity that comes from wellness, happiness, and collaborative work opportunities.

When it comes to deciding on the next office space, we shouldn't be looking for the lowest cost alternative or lowest rent. We should be searching for the space that best suits the vision of what our company does, what it stands for, and how it hopes to pass that message on to employees and to the community.

The ideal space isn't the least expensive one. It's the one that you can see yourself in for at least ten years because: it serves as an extension of your company's cultural values; an enhancement of your brand; a tool to help attract and retain talented people; a sustainable and efficient environment; a means to promote health and wellbeing for your people; and a collaborative, inspiring, agile, innovative, communal, and ultimately productive space that everyone who contributes to your company can be proud to call their workplace. With all these benefits comes greater profits.

CHAPTER 9

SUSTAINABLE SPACE: GREEN IS ALSO THE COLOR OF MONEY

"When you're surrounded by people who share a passionate commitment around a common purpose, anything is possible."
- Howard Schultz

Since we're discussing the all-important *money* portion of the RPM model, the subject of sustainability might at first seem a little counterintuitive. And we also need to put aside our political views about human-caused global warming. What matters is that moving toward sustainable practices and materials isn't about saving the environment. Saving the environment is a *side effect.* When it comes to your office space and management practices, sustainability is about both *saving* and *making* you money.

We'll get into those money factors in a moment, but first, let's also consider the personnel and customer benefits of going green. Belief that global warming is a threat to human life is at a three-decade high, a data point that means more people are paying attention to this stuff, so if you want to engender their loyalty, you need to be paying attention to it too.[1] It matters to future generations to the point where they are willing to spend more money on products and services provided by companies that demonstrate sustainable practices. In fact, in a global poll from 2015, 73% of these generations expressed a preference for sustainable companies, even if it meant paying more. Incidentally, in 2014, that number was only 50%, so you can see the trendline.

Additionally, on the recruitment and retention front, 83% of Millennials express that they would be more loyal to a company that allows them to contribute to social and environmental causes, 75% of them would take a pay cut to work for a socially responsible company, and 76% of them consider a company's social and environmental commitments

1 Gallup Poll. "Global Warming Concern at Three-Decade High." March 14, 2017.

Photo: Rice Energy (currently EQT) – Architectural design by NEXT Architecture, photo by Denmarsh Studios.

a strong motivating factor in deciding whether to work for them.[2] And it's not just Millennials. 90% of MBAs from business schools in Europe and North America prefer working for organizations committed to social responsibility.[3] Further, according to the CBRE report, "Wellness in the Workplace: Unlocking Future Performance," an estimated 80% of employees across all industries stated that a company's focus on wellness helped tip the scales in favor of recruiting or retaining them.[4]

So, as the workforce continues its rapid generational shift, the question of whether an employer can show engagement to the causes of sustainability and wellness is only going to matter more and more. For our office space, the most obvious (and surprisingly, one of the most cost-effective) causes to pursue is sustainable construction and building management practices. Sustainability is as much about quality of the materials you select to use in your office space—whether during construction, renovation, or upgrade—as it is about how you run your company. And this can be done whether you believe in global warming or not.

HAPPINESS + PRODUCTIVITY = VALUE

The world's most successful companies are already on the bandwagon. Amazon, Walmart, Coca-Cola, and HP are getting ahead of the curve here. Whether their leaders genuinely believe in human-caused global warming is irrelevant. What's relevant is that all these companies pour massive amounts of money into R&D for not just their products, but to their business practices, as well. Given the strides they have taken in recent years to run more environmentally friendly companies, it's clear what all that R&D is telling them. They have seen a need to demonstrate to the public that they are willing to make changes to reduce their environmental impact.

"But those are just big companies," you might be saying. It's true, the four companies I mentioned are some of the highest market-cap

---

2 Cone Communications. "Millennial Employee Engagement Study." 2016.

3 Montgomery, David B. and Ramus, Catherine A. "Corporate Social Responsibility Reputation Effects on MBA Job Choice." Stanford Graduate School of Business Working Paper No. 1805. July 29, 2003.

4 https://www.cbre.us/global/agile-real-estate/healthier-office-greater-productivity

companies in the world. But their examples apply to companies of all sizes, because every company wants to recruit top talent, drive productivity, and make more money, and as these companies show, demonstrating sustainable practices does *all* of these things.

But how? Their lush real estate and their cushy campuses are a huge factor, to be certain. Their cultures make for cohesive staffs. Google has the yoga classes and free childcare and the sleeping pods. The food in their cafeterias is supposed to be amazing. But the question we have to ask ourselves in this chapter is, do you think they do all this because they're trying to be nice? Sure, giving their employees a better quality of work-life blend is a good thing, but the truth is that they do all this because they want to drive productivity.

"Increasing connectivity, providing communal spaces, and giving chances to interact make a huge difference in productivity," said Dan Adamski of JLL. "But the buildings our clients are looking for also allow them to enjoy the productivity gains we've seen in sustainable spaces."

In chapter 6, we discussed how a focus on wellness can heighten worker engagement and productivity across the board. Well, the same is true for sustainability. Some of that has to do with pride in the workplace, but a lot of it has to do with the intriguing effect of how conservation of resources can help make everything a company does more efficient, including the way its employees work. These efforts to get better with energy and water use, to cut down on waste, and to use materials that make less of an impact on the environment also improve your people's quality of life. And as we've seen, if you improve the quality of their life, they're happier, and if they're happier, they work harder. In this way, the money you input into sustainable practices you make back many times over.

The other thing we have to keep in mind with these large companies is that they aren't following these practices just for the sake of following them. They have stakeholders to satisfy. On the subject of the amenities they offer, if they want to provide free bananas, they can't just set them out. They have to go in front of their boards and defend the bananas. So why are they giving all these perks? Because their boards see the value in the productivity they drive. The same is true for their environmental practices.

Why do you think that is? Why do you think all the highest market-cap companies are opting to follow more sustainable construction, maintenance, and management practices? Sure, some of them genuinely care about the environment, and some fear global warming, but the one main reason is that their stakeholders appreciate sustainability.

Their stakeholders appreciate sustainability, by the way, because companies that adhere to these practices tend to be more valuable. According to the Wildlife Fund, 53 of the Fortune 100 companies reported a savings of $1.1 billion annually through energy efficiency.[5] Further, "93 percent of corporate CEOs say that sustainability will be critical to the future success of their companies."[6] These CEOs and their stakeholders recognize that this is not just the right thing to do to attract more customers, but the right thing to do to save money and attract the most talented people.

The leaders of these companies see this cultural movement as an opportunity to evolve their *brand*. It's that old adage in brand management: evolve or go extinct. The other old adage is that branding is about trust. People pay more for brands because they trust them. I always buy Advil over the generic ibuprofen because I know that Advil has come through for me in the past. I trust Advil. Incidentally, 91% of Millennials said they would be more likely to place their trust in a brand that was associated with a cause.[7] And no matter what generation we're talking about, a large (and growing) number of people are more likely to place their trust in companies that do right by the environment. So, as the demand for sustainability rises, will you rise to become a more sustainable company?

It's just like the question of investment in the quality of your office space, and in your technology. If you're going to keep up with the

---

5 Baker, Bryn. "Leading By Example, Saving Millions." Worldwildlife.org. June 19, 2014.
6 Accenture. "Chief Executives Believe Overwhelmingly That Sustainability Has Become Critical to their Success, And Could Be Fully Embedded Into Core Business Within Ten Years." June 22, 2010.
7 Cone Communications. "Millennial CSR Study." 2015.

competition, then the only constant that you can count on is the need for change. Your practices must be environmentally sustainable if you're going to appeal to the majority of the talent pool, yes, but your organization *itself* must also be sustainable. It must be in position to evolve, change, and thrive with those changes. If you aren't fluid, adaptable, and agile, and if the brand of your office space isn't sending the right message, then you're going to get left behind.

REVENUE = AIR
GROWTH = WATER

Today, the best brands belong to the companies that demonstrate a commitment to doing the right thing—by their profit, by their people, and by their planet. It's John Elkington's Triple Bottom Line (TBL) in brand format. In previous chapters, we discussed how to do the right thing for your people. Ensure visual and posture comfort. Promote health and wellness (in the air, water, sound, food, fitness, and light quality, as well as in your cultural practices). Use your physical space to create a sense of community, collaboration, and freedom where everyone can take pride in their jobs. Seek feedback on every component of your office space. Embrace the work-life blend and the growing need for some flexibility between work and leisure time. Be fair, proud, generous, and always do the right thing. All of these strategies help improve not just the working lives of the people you count on, but their overall life satisfaction, as well. In these ways, we meet what I would argue is the key component of the TBL. We satisfy our people, who then in turn are better positioned to satisfy the people we serve. That goes a long way toward satisfying the profit component of the TBL, as well.

But the profit component actually has two major factors at play: revenue and growth. Revenue is like oxygen—if you cut it off, the business dies pretty quickly. Growth, meanwhile, is like water. The business can survive without it for a little while, but not nearly as long as you would think. To ensure a consistent source of that water that is growth, then we as business leaders must seek to maximize our return on every investment. Every dollar spent must be leveraged toward the effort of growing the business. Anything less is just a waste of money, and just another day without water.

DELTA POINT:
BUILDING SUSTAINABLY IS ***LESS EXPENSIVE***

According to a poll by Dodge Data & Analytics, the primary obstacle to the decision to build a sustainable office space is higher perceived first costs.[8] In fact, in the US, 70% of business leaders polled believed that it costs more. And it's easy to see why. Five to ten years ago, that statement was absolutely true. It used to cost more (and sometimes substantially more) to build or upgrade to a more sustainable workplace. But by popular demand, the competition has thickened, and that has driven the prices down to where it simply does not cost more up front to build with better controls, more resource-friendly materials, energy saving glass, low VOC (volatile organic compounds) paints, chemicals, and carpet resins, and so on. In part for these reasons, 60% of commercial construction starts worldwide are projected to be sustainable projects in 2018.[9] This is a figure that has doubled every three years since 2012, so the trendline is clear.

So they're comparatively inexpensive to build, and they're popular. You know what else? Sustainable buildings appreciate at a higher rate and hold their value longer than their traditional counterparts. If you're thinking about buying or renting a building, you're just far more likely to choose the one that has the latest technology—and the latest technology is almost always sustainable. It's that "shiny new penny" principle. If something seems to be closer to the cutting edge of technology, it's going to retain value for longer. Add in the benefit of knowing that this building is going to meet with public approval, and that it's going to cost less to operate, so the investment will return long-term.

It's like I always say: new buildings win, old buildings lose. Sure, there are old buildings that can be gutted and updated to the point where they become new-old buildings. I've seen plenty of fifty-year-

8 Lyons Hardcastle, Jessica. "Lower Operating Cost Is No. 1 Reason to Build Green, 'Perceived' Higher Cost is Biggest Obstacle." Environmental Leader. February 18, 2016.
9 Ibid.

old spaces that have been gutted and rebuilt with every one of these cultural and professional amenities we've been discussing up to this point. But we're already facing a building boom in this country, and that trend is only going to continue.

Demographic and cultural shifts are already delivering us to a point where there is an awful lot of tired and obsolete real estate out there. Some of it could be gutted and rebuilt, but most of it would be better off coming down. If we're talking about a progressive company that wants to gain advantages over the competition and win the talent war, then it's time to recognize this revolutionary trend. It's time for new buildings, sustainable buildings, buildings with all the bells and whistles that will be easily upgradable to new technologies and hold their value longer. Given the minor cost differences between building new and gutting the old, and considering what amounts to a surprisingly small investment relative to a general and administrative expense budget, new construction is almost always the better play.

At the end of the day, whichever path you take, there must be a commitment to sustainability if you're going to keep up with the competition. You have to look past that assumption that it's going to cost more, and recognize that it's actually going to cost the same (or less) while saving you significant money and holding more value in the long run.

That value is a key point that I should emphasize. I'm not a consultant or researcher, after all; I'm a business leader. So I'm all about value. New buildings tend to have the best technologies, and the majority of them run on sustainable practices, which means they operate for far less, and they tend to contribute to the wellness and happiness of the staff that winds up occupying them. It's the difference between an economy and luxury car. People are willing to pay more for the latter, because they'll be more comfortable and will enjoy better performance while driving the car.

MANAGING YOUR SPACE SUSTAINABLY SAVES A *TON* OF MONEY

There was a time when the popular belief was that the cost for being more environmentally friendly was prohibitive. Only the biggest, best capitalized companies could possibly afford it. But times have changed.

These days, building and renovating with sustainable practices is often less expensive than going the traditional route, and assuming you then properly engage in sustainable management practices, you save a ton of money in both the short- and long-term. It used to be that the argument was, "Sure, this stuff costs more, but it pays for itself over time." Now it's more like, "It's less expensive now, and it starts saving you money immediately. Why would you not do this?"

So you're considering upgrading to sustainable office space. That's good. Your people, and the public, will appreciate it. What's better is that your electric, water, and gas bills are going to go way, way down. Yes, some of the strategies for getting your space running on more sustainable practices will require a little up-front investment, but if you're committed to upgrading your space anyway, then we're no longer talking about spending money just for the sake of looking more sustainable. We're talking about making the right choices on product selection.

For instance, LED bulbs are slightly more expensive than their traditional counterparts, but they are also 75% more energy efficient, and they need to be changed far less often—which saves you on the electricity bill and the replacement/installation bill. In some states, you might be able to benefit from tax incentives, as well. Couple them with motion-activated light switches to ensure that unoccupied rooms aren't burning through your electric bill. The daylight harvesting controls I mentioned in chapter 6 can save you significant money. If you're thinking bigger, solar panels might sound expensive, but the costs come down every year, the savings over the long-term are incredible, and in many places, you receive federal and local tax benefits to install them.

On the subject of energy management and conservation, start by installing an HVAC with a strong Energy Star rating. Install smart thermostats that adjust temperatures automatically based on the weather outside. New energy management systems can be operated easily and remotely, as well, so that tends to save on the expenses related to service calls. At the Bentley, the controls are so seamless that a manager can be sitting at home and use his smartphone to change the temperature of the building.

On the water management front, change out the plants in your office and patio space with plants that don't require as much irrigation. Invest in re-grading toward irrigation swells, so you never need to run an irrigation system again. Inside, in the bathrooms, consider installing low-flow toilets and energy efficient hand dryers.

Have your cleaning staff use environmentally friendly chemicals and clean during the day instead of at night. I can't stress that last point enough. At Burns Scalo, we're finding significant savings in switching from night-cleaning to day-cleaning. If you still have your cleaning staff visit your office at night, just think about what that's costing you on electricity to keep the lights on and the temperature at 70 for that extra eight hours. Bring them in during the day instead, and they're cleaning when the lights are already on and the temperature is set to a comfortable level. As an added benefit, the daytime staffs at cleaning companies tend to be more personable and trustworthy in general, so you save on theft, as well.

It might seem like having a cleaning staff on site during the day could be distracting, but you'd be amazed at how these companies can map out a plan that minimizes disruption. Soon after hiring our daytime cleaning staff, it didn't just get to where most people didn't even notice their work, but they also started to feel like a part of our corporate family. The relationships are overwhelmingly positive—so positive that it makes sense to think of your cleaning staff as an extension to your management team. Think about it. Who else in the organization observes a higher percentage of your space every day? The cleaning staff goes *everywhere.* So there is no one better to tell you when there is a problem or an opportunity for an upgrade. Returning to the sustainability initiative, consider planting more trees and gardens and potted flowers outside the building. Increase the number of potted plants around the office, as well, for a boost to the air quality and wellness quotient. Consider installing more energy efficient windows or treating and reinforcing the insulation of your existing windows to help cut down on the electricity and heating bills and lower your carbon footprint. In many cases, these efforts can also secure you a federal and local tax break.

The list of straightforward, relatively simple upgrades is a long one, and it all depends on what you're willing to invest. But again, that investment pays you back in public goodwill, savings on the utilities, and sometimes even tax benefits or credits. Whatever you decide, before you start making the investment, the best way to figure out how to maximize your return is to run an energy management study to determine the best systems for your unique energy consumption profile.

It also helps to hire someone to retro-commission your electrical and HVAC systems, and also check your insulation, structural integrity, and windows. The best plan is of course the most comprehensive, and the message is most powerful when you're sincere about the effort. But for anyone who remains hesitant to make these kinds of upgrades in a wholehearted fashion, there are at least smaller steps to pursue between now and 2030. The more you commit to on this front, the more competitive you'll be when the talent war peaks. And remember, it's not as expensive up front as you think it is, and the long-term savings will more than make up for the discomfort.

THIRD-PARTY ENDORSEMENTS ENHANCE THE TRUST-FACTOR

At Burns Scalo, we believe in naming our buildings because it helps contribute to the building's brand. When we were constructing the office in which the company now resides, we spent a lot of time brainstorming the name for the building. We knew that it was going to be the most luxurious space in the corridor, and would have the highest-end features and technology. As a result, we also knew that it was likely to be the highest priced building in the submarket. Getting people into the right mindset about this space would be a matter of borrowing the equity from a similarly expensive and luxurious brand. Hence the name, "The Bentley," and for that matter, the names of some of our other buildings, like "The Riviera," "Stealth Technology Center," "The Fountainhead," "The Dakota," and "The Boardwalk."

On a similar note, early in my tenure of running Burns Scalo, we began a promotion where we give away Rolex watches as a reward for great performance. Now, we could give away just about anything, but we chose Rolex because the brand is so widely recognizable for its quality. More specifically, we chose Rolex because it allowed us to borrow their brand equity. When most people hear Rolex, that quality is the first thing that comes to mind. If we'd wanted people to think, "good value with reasonable prices," we might have given away Seiko watches and named our building, "The Chevy." But instead, we intended our audience to associate Burns Scalo with other high-quality brands.

This is, of course, not a new or original concept. Companies borrow equity from other brands all the time. I raise this story to point out that, on the sustainability front, the easiest way to benefit from exactly this same strategy is to seek third-party endorsements on the quality of your office space. Branding, after all, is a long-term process. It's not a matter of selling someone on an idea; it's a matter of building a legacy and projecting long-term value. So, while pursuing LEED[10], WELL[11], and/or Class-G[12] certification isn't absolutely essential to the message that you're committed to sustainable practices, being able to install a third-party plaque on your office space announces to the world that you have a good space that meets the standards you're claiming to set. People trust LEED, WELL, and Class-G (which, full disclosure, is a management process checklist that I founded and co-own) as brands, and so third-party endorsements like these allow you to borrow that brand equity and literally display it on your door. They announce to the world—and more specifically, to your people, your recruits, and your customers—that the experts on the subject of sustainability are endorsing you for doing the right thing.

Again, third-party certification isn't a *requirement* in the commercial office space market—and some of them are impractical for certain businesses or offices to pursue—but they certainly help enhance the brand, which in turn enhances the value of your company, which very clearly speaks to the "M" in "RPM."

After we started building and managing LEED-certified projects at Burns Scalo, it soon came to light that some businesses were making the right

10 https://new.usgbc.org/leed
11 https://www.wellcertified.com/
12 https://www.class-g.org/

decisions for sustainable materials and systems, but then weren't actually running their buildings the right way. They would have all the bells and whistles required to reduce their energy bills, but then they would leave the lights on all night. Or they would have all these nice irrigation swells, and would run their irrigation systems anyway.

This was why I founded Class-G. Whether you're in a new building or an old one, Class-G provides a management process checklist that you can follow to make sure you're running your office space in a way that not only ensures you're following sustainable practices, but also maximizes the potential for its design. The checklist looks at your specific space and shows you how to run your systems in the most efficient (and cost-effective) way possible. Where LEED is that gold star for your construction practices, Class-G is the gold star for your management practices. As a benefit, it also helps you figure out how to use your existing systems to save you the most money.

Meanwhile, WELL is a certification for that other key component of the TBL: people. WELL utilizes an evidence-based process to measure and monitor how your space impacts the health and wellness of the people who occupy it. In short, just as we discussed in chapter 6, it measures the quality of the air, the water, the light, and the food you provide, while also assessing the overall comfort and fitness (both physical and mental) opportunities available in the space. It is more difficult to make an existing space meet WELL standards without committing to a thorough renovation, but if you're constructing a new space, there is no better third-party endorsement for your commitment to the health and wellness of your people.

DON'T MISS THE SUSTAINABILITY WAVE

As I said at the outset, the time has come to put aside politics and disregard personal feelings. Sustainability is no longer a costly investment to protect the environment, and wellness initiatives are no longer touchy-feely efforts to appeal to the under-30 set. They aren't just the wave of the future either. They are very much in the now. Recruits from the younger generations are already asking questions about sustainable practices, about light and air quality, and about whether you're committed to doing the right thing for the planet and your people.

And in the coming years, as more and more of them reach working age, you'd better have a good answer to these questions.

Having more efficient lighting, appliances, controls, glass, and so on might represent an investment up front, but even if it costs a little more, we're still just talking about things you were going to have to spend money on regardless. You're going to need to replace your lightbulbs and appliances eventually. If we're talking about even-money on the replacements, it's a no-brainer. Go sustainable. But even if we're talking about 10% or 20% more for some products, is that slightly higher cost really so important that you would risk losing all the benefits we've discussed in this chapter?

If we're talking about constructing, renovating, or moving into a more sustainable space where you can expect productivity to rise by as much as 50%, then what does it matter if the rent will be 10% or 20% higher? Spend a little more, get a lot more. Absorb the incidental costs, and the savings and benefits in the long-term will be considerable. In the end, the savings will become somewhat incidental, as well, because you'll be too busy basking in the people and profit benefits. You really can't put a price on what you gain in culture, brand, customer response, and the satisfaction and productivity of your staff.

UPMC

CHAPTER 10

HOW TO MAXIMIZE THE RETURN ON YOUR NEXT OFFICE

"Success doesn't happen to you. It happens because of you."
- Grant Cardone

With this chapter, we're going to be discussing how to conduct your next office search in a way that maximizes your return on investment. To get there, we'll examine all three of our case study companies—the former startup, Blattner Brunner, Inc., an integrated marketing firm that grew to dominate its market; the mid-sized company, Waldron Private Wealth, a nationally rated financial services firm; and the large company, Rice Energy, recently cited as one of the most rapidly growing companies in the US and even more recently sold to EQT for a high multiple. Their stories about how they arrived in their most recent office spaces will impart lessons about how to connect your office design to your culture and enjoy spectacular productivity from your staff (and revenues to boost your bottom line) as a result.

BUY-IN IS KEY

I've mentioned already that Blattner Brunner, Inc., embarked on several office moves over the course of their climb to the top of the Pittsburgh market. Because they moved so often, they make for a nice case study on what to do *and* what not to do. As founder Joe Blattner put it, having the right *intentions* about your space isn't necessarily enough. Yes, there are many advantages to open office plans with luxurious amenities and a concierge flair—but only if you plan the layout properly, examine every element through the productivity lens, and most importantly, get proper buy-in from your staff.

In 1994, when they made the leap to their first open office, they soon learned that not involving the staff in the process led to a few oversights with the planning. They kept the closed-door spaces for key executives, which is something Blattner has advocated against ever since. The same

Photo: The Riviera – Architectural design by NEXT Architecture.

goes for the five-foot-high panels surrounding the staff workspaces. "It was horrible," Blattner explained. "We had a pretty office building, but our space *wasn't*." For a company that hoped to inspire its clients with creative thinking, having an uninspiring office space didn't seem to fit. On top of that, the high panels and closed doors meant that no one could see each other while seated at their desks, and as we covered in chapter 6, they couldn't hear each other very well, either.

Again, part of these mistakes they owed to the notion that they were essentially pioneering the movement—particularly in Pittsburgh, a city relatively slow to adopt the transition to more open and inspiring spaces. But the other factors came from a personnel and financial perspective. "The staff was a little resistant to the idea of going to open space at first," Joe explained. "Some of their concerns probably could have helped us avoid some of the mistakes we made in that first design. But mostly we were just too focused on not spending money. If we had thought about productivity and buy-in first and expense second, we might have seen some of these problems coming."

In 1998, with the lease on their uninspiring space coming to an end, they took their first step toward fixing those problems. Despite some resistance from employees who were at first exasperated by the noise levels and relative lack of privacy, Blattner and Brunner were both fully on board with continuing the open-space plan, provided they could learn from the past and evolve. And so, Blattner led the charge toward a new design based on staff input.

"Our business was getting some traction," he explained. "And overall, we were beginning to think about being best-of-class in everything we were doing." The company hired an architect to help rethink everything about how an office could be designed. After extensive research, coupled with the trial and error from the previous building, they realized that the process had to be led by connecting management to staff, opening sightlines to improve culture and productivity, inviting collaboration through shared space, and of course, the all-important sound attenuation. The result was a much more *functional* office that retained and even improved upon the Wow Factor from the first space. Just as importantly, the staff, having seen their needs met more completely, were much happier in this new office.

For Waldron Private Wealth, seeking buy-in from the staff was a slightly more challenging matter. In the financial services industry, professionals tend to favor more traditional office concepts. "It was clear to everyone we had to move so we could all be in the same space," founder John Waldron said. "But for most of us, before we began this process, we were too focused on how things were always done. We were too used to our traditional, closed-door offices. Many of the staff didn't see the appeal of moving to a space with fewer walls. Part of it was that we weren't thinking about what the space could do for our culture. We were more focused on client service and business development. As long as the office was functional, we were fine with it."

But then, when John began to think about and prioritize the design of his company's next office space, he recognized the many ways that such an investment can pay off. "As we went through the process and started to educate ourselves, we found that real estate really helps drive your culture, message, and brand. The more we got into it, the more we realized that this was absolutely something we had to pay attention to, because if we got it right, it could be a huge asset for us."

The trick, though, was getting everybody on board to an open office. "We were hearing that people liked the privacy of their own office," John said. "There was a certain amount of stature attached to having your name on a door. After we pitched the open plan to them, we heard some pushback around the water cooler. The general reaction was that everything was going to be turned upside down and they would all be in this loud, distracting space."

Some leaders in John's shoes might have taken this as a sign that they shouldn't be pursuing a move toward a space with the Wow Factor. Some might have just figured that you need to give the staff what they want, and in the end, no matter what you design, what matters most is that it's *new.* Fortunately, John recognized that the benefits he had uncovered in his research were worth pushing for. "It's like anything when it comes to change," he said. "People don't like change. And everyone we talked to in the real estate industry said that we were going to have pushback. It's only natural."

To overcome the resistance, John did something really insightful. He formed a real estate transition committee to help design and plan the new space, and he staffed the committee with the biggest naysayers and detractors on the staff. By making them part of the process, the people who used to be the most vocal opponents of this idea began to buy in because they had that pride of authorship. Rather than having to accept John's word about the benefits and just hope for the best, now they were speaking directly with the consultants and design engineers, and seeing firsthand how great the new concept would be. "That was probably the best decision we made," John said. "Because it made them want to be a part of the move."

When you run a mid-sized firm, it's one thing to seek input and buy-in from the most vocal naysayers, but what if you're running a giant company staffed by hundreds or even thousands of people? At Rice Energy, when it quickly became apparent that the central office they had only just moved into six months ago wasn't going to be big enough to support their rapid growth, seeking buy-in for another move—this time into a building they would design and build from the ground up—was a much different story.

The executive team was quick to embrace the need, but for Jamie Rogers, the question was how to get enough of the staff thinking about the new building as more than just the place to go and sit at a desk. "The executive group and I spent a lot of time working on this question," Jamie explained. "We knew that we couldn't just work on solving the tangible problem of needing more space. We also had to figure out how to refocus our employees on creating the kind of place where they actually *wanted* to work. It's tough to get people to accept change. But at the same time, people translate space to worth. We knew that if we solicited enough feedback, and we gave people a respectable work area that they enjoyed spending time in, it would help reduce resistance to the move."

GIVE MORE, GET MORE

By 2000, it was time once again for Blattner Brunner, Inc., to move, and this time they would make their first leap into a Class-A downtown space. The firm found a long-term, abandoned space in one of the highest quality buildings in downtown Pittsburgh, and they struck a huge deal with the departing occupants Westinghouse that came with a $1.6 million renovation allowance. The renovation allowance and some of the firm's own capital to work with put them in design heaven. Now, for the first time in their history, they could create a best-in-class space to match their best-in-class aspirations.

By this point, it was clear that open office *worked,* but only if you sought ways to harness the beneficial collaboration without adding to the productivity-hindering distraction. This time, they could continue to implement all the elements they had learned they couldn't live without, and with the bigger budget, could give their staff more amenities and perks than ever before.

They returned with the white noise, and added fabrics, walls, ceilings, floors, and technologies that all attenuated sound. They kept the height of their partitions to four feet, which ensured that people wouldn't speak too loudly while also encouraging interaction and promoting productivity.

Those all-important sightlines continued into the conference rooms, as well, where the walls were constructed of floor to ceiling glass. Each room made for highly collaborative space—space that invited brainstorming and innovation through white boards, pushpin walls, and presentation monitors. Since they were a company that depended on advertising creativity, they were one of the first anywhere to hang TV monitors all around the office. "Our product was media," Blattner said. "So art alone on the walls didn't do it for us. We ran news channels or music videos on those TVs 24-7, with copy tags streaming below." They would leave the TVs muted, but the visual stimulation helped drive creativity.

They extended the open concept to the offices of leadership, as well. Even the owners of the company occupied offices that were partially open. The partitions around their workspaces were six feet high, but there were no doors. "My belief was that we would benefit from full transparency," Blattner explained. "Top to bottom, bottom to top."

During this final design process, Blattner brought a singular philosophy way ahead of its time. The benefits of open space had already made themselves apparent, but what he saw way back in 2000 was that if you **give more, you get more**. Long before anyone was talking about work-life blend, Blattner was ensuring that his staff, his clients, his prospects, and any guests who visited the office would feel as if they had all their needs met.

And in return for all that giving, productivity skyrocketed. Billability, profitability, the number of productive hours spent on progressing client projects to where they could get them out the door—all of these measures took giant leaps. Those gains Blattner Brunner shared with the staff. In all staff meetings, they would promote how they were progressing profit-wise, and preach the message that everyone benefits from this hard work.

"We made sure that everyone always knew about our productivity," Joe said. "We wanted them to see that we appreciated their hard work, and we were rewarding it with profit sharing, but also with the perks in the office. The message was that we weren't trying to work them to death. We were working them to *life*. We wanted them to be productive and billable, but we also wanted them to be comfortable and actually *want* to be in the office." The contrast between Blattner Brunner and other firms, where the tendency is to work staff to the bone, was stark. Yes, there was hard work happening in this new office, but it was also lively and enjoyable.

For John Waldron, it was never a question about whether giving more would lead to greater returns; the question that evolved for him was how *much* more they would give. "We started out with a functional budget for the project," he explained, "but when we realized that this was more than just a *functional* opportunity, and was in fact an *identity* opportunity, we effectively doubled our budget." John admits that the investment was a little tough to swallow at first, but the more he and his team learned, the more they recognized the new space as an opportunity to promote who they were and what they stood for as a company.

So the real estate transition team began looking at architectural design firms. Once they had seen all the presentations and chosen their architect, they got down to the work of determining various directions to take the design. Every iteration of the design delivered more feedback on what was important to the staff. "With every decision," John said, "the energy started to lift a little more. The team was involved in every phase of the development, and that allowed them to see *why* we were making these choices. There was a give and take with the design firms, and they saw the evolution of the design. It was a long process, but by the time it was done, everyone saw the specifics of what we were giving them, and there was really no resistance after that."

So the feedback drove the process, but it also led to the perfect opportunity for the staff to see firsthand how much John cared about their comfort and wellbeing at work. "The ROI on office space investment is infinite if you include the whole organization in the process," John said. "If you get their input, you're not just making a real estate investment; you're investing in your team and your culture." And as Waldron Private Wealth has seen in the years since, that investment pays off in recruiting and retention, staff cohesion and productivity, and the bottom line.

THE WORKSPACE MESSAGE

For Rice Energy, a company challenging the status quo of an industry, the ultimate goal was to do the same thing with their building. "We wanted the building to be more than just bricks and mortar and where people would sit at their desks," Jamie Rogers explained. "We wanted it to be a place where people actually *want* to be—a place that promotes our values as a company and also shows that we respect our employees."

As Jamie soon learned, this is no easy task when you're trying to do that for a company with so many employees. "Even taking a company public paled in comparison to the effort that had to go into creating a 150,000 square foot space that could meet the needs of so many different roles. The decisions you're making along the way are going to impact every single person in the company."

So the Rice Energy transition team focused their attention on figuring out how to design an office that would be reflective of how they wanted their employees to work. "In the final design," Jamie said, "private offices only went to people at the director level or above, so in the entire company, we're only talking about sixty to seventy private offices. We dedicated tons of collaboration space—and I don't mean conference rooms. Some areas have defined conference rooms, but otherwise, a lot of it is open collaboration areas where people can just sit down and talk and work together."

The ultimate message was that they weren't investing in this new building just to create more space that they could grow into, but rather, "It refocused our employees on how we wanted them to work. More importantly, it reinforced the message that we respect them. When you're constantly growing out of offices and people are moving and sharing offices, that doesn't send the best message about how the executive level feels about the employees. People see their space as a reflection of how they should work, so in those situations, employees just see their space being marginalized."

This isn't to say that space can't be a consideration. "It's not like we went and gave everyone egregiously large offices," Jamie explained. "What we did was give people a respectable work area. Some people did go from offices in the old building to workstations in the new one, but these workstations were anything but your traditional cube."

The workstations at the mostly open floor plans at Rice Energy are low-walled to take advantage of those sightline and collaboration benefits. Everyone has a power-operated, height-adjustable desk that allows them to sit or stand, depending on their preferences. About that, Jamie makes an important point: "The stationary desks versus height-adjustable were fairly comparable in price, so there wasn't any kind of angle being played here. It wasn't a cost thing. We had a choice, so we opted to give our people the choice about how they would want to work."

At Blattner Brunner, even back in 2000, the workspaces were what we would still call innovative today. Arranged into pods that the company lovingly referred to as "six-packs," staff would situate themselves in sets of six workstations. Four would align along the perimeter. While there was slightly less privacy in these spaces, they also had the advantage of being closer to the windows. The other two workspaces resided in the inner core of the pod, facing toward one another with a single high-top meeting table for collaborative sessions between them.

In some pods, the managers would take these spaces, but not in all of them. The message was clear: these are all attractive workspaces of equal quality. Where the employee chose to set up shop had nothing to do with job title, but rather, with personal preference. If he or she wanted more privacy, then the inner core made sense. If he/she preferred a window, then one of the other four desks would suit them. All told, there were 144 workspaces, and not one bad seat in the house.

On the subject of those seats, one of the bigger expenses was the decision to give everyone an airplane cable Herman Miller chair. Back in 2000, these were the highest-end office chairs, and any of the staff who looked up the cost of them would wonder why they bothered spending $1,000 on each of these office chairs when they could have instead passed that money on to the staff in the form of raises. "I told them I wasn't doing it to be nice," Blattner said. "I told them we spent the money because I wanted them to be so comfortable that they would sit in those chairs for hours, working hard and making this company a ton of money. And they would laugh and drop the matter."

For Waldron Private Wealth, the message really came into focus the moment the staff first saw the designs tangibly come together. "When they saw the color palettes on the walls and the glass going in and the furniture getting set up," John said, "*that's* when they started to understand why we were doing this. We were doing it for them. We wanted them to be as comfortable and happy in their space as they could be." Sending a message that you want your staff to be comfortable and happy has since benefitted Waldron Private Wealth—as it would for any company—in that the message about the quality of workspace has translated into the quality of work being done in those spaces.

"The cross-section of our staff that didn't see the benefits of this really started to see it about a month before we moved in," John explained. "And then after we moved in, everything changed for the better. These open workspaces got people talking to each other and collaborating in ways they never did before. And all our collaborative and recreational spaces changed the way they interacted. I'm the only one in the building with a private office, and frankly I don't like being in the office. I feel like I'm on the sidelines and not in the game with everybody else."

To help drive home the message that this is a place that believes in the work-life blend, the Waldron design team decided to name the conference rooms and breakout rooms after popular vacation spots like Aspen, Tahoe, Hawaii, and of course, the Grand Cayman Room. "There's an energy that comes from these kinds of environments," John explained. "You just can't help but want to be part of it."

DON'T FORGET THE FOOD

At the Beacon, a huge amount of that energy flows around the beautiful café that serves as one of the office's two main hubs. With a state of the art food preparation area and plenty of space that can be converted for dining or hosting, the café isn't just a place for the staff to enjoy the gourmet food on hand, but also a place to host genuinely awe-inspiring events. The café reinforces the message that Waldron Private Wealth wants to ensure the health and happiness of its employees while also encouraging plenty of cross-talk and interaction both during the average workday and during any function the company hosts for clients and prospects.

The other hub, known as the Grand Cayman room, plays host to a different but equally inviting vibe. "You don't see many financial services offices with this kind of room," John said. "But when we were designing, we said let's create this really beautiful conference space, and then let's maybe put a pool table in here and a bar."

The result is a room that meets a number of key duties in a truly inspiring way. Clients are invited to wait in this space. They host larger meetings here. And during events, people tend to gravitate to the coolest space in the building. "People are really enthusiastic about it." This is in part because it's so beautifully designed and so outside the norm for a financial services company, but also because people associate so many positive feelings with food and drink. It's just like any great restaurant or bar. The food is important, but so is the environment. At Waldron Private Wealth, between the café and the Grand Cayman room, they have created two environments that create plenty of buzz.

At the newly renovated downtown space for Blattner Brunner, Inc., the food-related messaging started with the town-square-style café that served as the central hub of the office. The Wow Factor of this space centered around the beautiful, curvilinear coffee bar that extended thirty feet through the center. The S-shaped surface was of smooth wood with inspiring arcs and creative flair. It wasn't just a place to sit and eat lunch or drink coffee—it was the coffee bar of an innovative marketing firm. Here, people could gather for impromptu meetings, collaborate, entertain, and be inspired.

"We wanted to have this common space that signaled who we were as a firm," Blattner said. "We wanted people to enjoy the idea of eating and meeting and collaborating together." To this end, they never allowed spaces like the town square to just rest unused. They brought in food regularly, providing snacks and lunch and sparing no expense to help their employees and visitors meet this crucial need. "You look now at how much companies like Google and Uber are spending in terms of time and energy and money on feeding their people. It's mindboggling how much they focus on it, and it's also mindboggling how much the investment pays off."

The benefits of enticing people with food in the office go well beyond making sure they're properly fed. It encourages cross-talk and collaboration. Suddenly, clients and partners and prospects wanted to spend more time in the Blattner Brunner offices. This ramped up productivity, as employees rarely had to travel out of the building for meetings or lunch. The town square wasn't just the center of the space—it became the center of everything the company did. In this way, the money spent on food and drink paid for itself in the returns gained by the drastic improvement in productivity and availability of staff.

For Rice Energy, the message was clear, but the question was how do you provide inviting eateries and food on such a grand scale? "We knew we wanted to provide a great space where people could eat in the building," Jamie Rogers said. "And we knew we wanted the food to be spectacular." So they partnered with a regional player to design their cafeteria and work out the logistics of providing healthy, delicious food that wasn't just more enticing, but more affordable, as well. They kept out the pizza ovens and fryers, focusing on healthier options. But the real message came from the decision to have the company subsidize a portion of the meal expense. "The cost was negligible compared to the happiness it brought to our employees. When you can choose from a huge and rotating selection of meals, and when you can get a gourmet sandwich for $3 for lunch, there's no reason to leave the building at that point."

You can see the benefit to the company baked right into that message. It's more of that give more, get more scenario. By making the investment to ensure that their cafeteria and the food it provided was more enticing than anything an employee could hope to find in the surrounding areas, they ensured that more people stayed in the building during lunch, which cut down on transition and commute times and translated into more time to be productive.

Further, by providing healthy options, the company ensured that more of its staff would be invigorated, instead of bogged down, by the food they ate. "It's just like with the gym," Jamie said. "If you encourage healthy behavior, you see those benefits in everyone's productivity. We are fervent believers that if you're running at 50% capacity in the early afternoon, then going and doing something physical is going to help you get back up closer to 100% productive again. It's why we spent so much of our budget on the gym. Food is that same way."

THE SEARCH TEAM

With all these lessons in mind, the question becomes how do you choose and design your ideal space? Burns Scalo's most successful clients have been advocates of assembling a search team to scout locations, set the buildout budget, and ultimately lead the planning and design phase. The ideal search team features at least two people: an executive to represent the needs and wants of leadership and a leader from HR to represent the needs and wants of the staff. This is of course the bare minimum. The more people—particularly creative people—from the various departments of your business whose input you can solicit, the better. In an effort to avoid the too-many-cooks-in-the-kitchen principle, not all of them should have the power to weigh in on every decision, but there is tremendous value in gathering input from all levels of the business. No matter where that input comes from, the end result should be that this decision came down to the opinions of more than one person.

According to Jamie Rogers, having a search team and a design committee was incredibly beneficial to the process. "If you have only one or two people at the executive level making these decisions," Jamie said, "how are they going to know what the twenty-four-year-old entry-level staffer is going to value in their space?" A key point, given that much of the day to day productivity in any given company is carried on the backs of those entry-level staffers. Seeking their input is paramount. "Consensus doesn't necessarily lead to agreement," Jamie warned, "but it gives people a chance to feel like their voices are heard." This, in turn, leads to everyone taking greater pride and ownership in the space that results from the search, design, and buildout.

THE PROGRAMMING EXERCISE

Given that they were growing so rapidly, Rice Energy began its programming exercise by examining hiring plans. The needs of every department. The vibe they wanted the space to project. They included in the discussion every VP and director-level person in the company. All input was welcome. "We wanted to have every department involved because they were closest to the head-count projections," Rogers said. "Mostly we just didn't want any of our departments to be out of line with the others—didn't want too many workspaces in one and too few in another. But ultimately their input extended well beyond the numbers. Their opinions drove most of the design process."

They began with a statistical analysis: how many people Rice Energy employed now, how many they planned to add, which areas they expected the business to grow the most versus the least, and so on. This portion of the show was more formulaic, an effort to ensure that we had the exact right number of seats for both present and future staff so that the company wouldn't run into a space issue again in the foreseeable future. This helped shape a preliminary picture for the footprint of each department and the makeup of every floor. With staff projections in hand, they could begin identifying space for the fitness center, the cafeteria, conference and auditorium space, and so on. During the programming exercise, you assemble all the pieces of the puzzle before figuring out how to fit them together.

OUTFITTING THE SPACE

It might sound like putting the cart before the horse, but once the program exercise is complete and the reports and recommendations assembled, the next step in the ideal strategy is to figure out how you're going to furnish the space you'll be occupying. At Rice Energy, the search team traveled to several office furniture design firms to get a handle on what they wanted the look and feel of the new Rice Energy building to be. "Before we toured these warehouses," Jamie Rogers said, "we didn't have a clear picture of how our space should look. We just knew we didn't want it to be a cubicle farm. You can tell when you walk into an office with six-foot-high cubicles that it isn't a place that sparks a whole lot of informal collaboration. We didn't want to be like that. We wanted our space to be open, so that people could see each other and interact."

The showrooms at these furniture companies feature tens of thousands of square feet of varied workspaces set up so you can actually see, feel, and experience what it would be like to work in one. In this way, you aren't simply relying on someone else to tell you what your staff might need; you're making a firsthand decision.

"If we had defaulted to what other people were telling us," Rogers said, "the result wouldn't have matched our culture. The way you furnish your space is an opportunity to differentiate your company in terms of culture and brand. It's a physical reflection of what your company stands for—an optical, tangible representation of how the management team views its staff, values them, and expects them to work. Why leave that opportunity in someone else's hands?"

The trip to interact with prospective workspaces in person also sparked a huge number of ideas that the search team hadn't considered before. Originally, they had a somewhat more conventional design in mind, but the end result was decidedly less so. The company operates in the wildly competitive oil and gas industry, but their design didn't wind up looking so much like a traditional oil and gas company. It had more of a modern-tech-company feel. Lots of conference rooms, but in unconventional spaces. Plenty of lounge seating. Endless opportunities to kick back and throw a presentation from a laptop onto a TV or projection screen.

"Once we took the leap of faith that our folks would want to work in an environment like that," Jamie said, "it was incredible the feedback we received." Thanks to the tour of the furniture showrooms, they settled on smaller workspaces for their staff than they had planned previously, but they were confident that their employees would respond favorably given the varied and shared spaces, the opportunities to interact, the healthy food they would be provided in the cafeteria, the high-end fitness center they would have access to, and so on. "We started off concerned about the individual workstation itself, but adding these other amenities changed all that. Ultimately our desire to create a positive total work experience outweighed the size of the space."

FINALIZING THE DESIGN

For Rice Energy, the process was remarkably smooth and quick. The planning started in December, with construction beginning in April. But really, once they had gotten feedback from all levels and departments, and once they had decided on workspace layout and amenities, the process became rather simple. Knowing what people wanted, coupled with a better sense of how the physical components of the build could communicate a sense that this was a comparatively young, refreshingly progressive, and highly driven organization, brought everything into sharp focus.

Some companies may face resistance to some of these more forward-thinking ideas, but with Rice Energy, deciding on the layout of the floorplates that would finalize the design was a matter of putting all the puzzle pieces together. Granted, with every floorplate 30,000 square feet in a building that covered five floors and 150,000 square feet, it was a rather *large* puzzle.

When asked why the picture was so much clearer for the Rice Energy team, Jamie Rogers didn't hesitate. "I think when you start out, the tendency is to think about space first, but what's more important is getting the *right* space. It's about finding or creating a physical representation of the company's culture and brand. The space can be one of the most powerful tools you have to reinforce the company's message."

At the end of the day, whether you're constructing a new building from the ground up, as Rice Energy did, constructing a space that houses your office and serves as a real estate investment, as Waldron Private Wealth did, or renovating an existing space to suit your needs, like Blattner Brunner, the way to maximize the return on your investment is to use it to reinforce what your company stands for, what you expect of your people, and how you want to be viewed by the public. If you get it right, everything (*everything*) improves.

"It's kind of silly how great this investment is," Jamie Rogers said. "Turnover reduces. Absenteeism drops. You wind up in a healthier, more enjoyable, more engaging place to work. All of this contributes to a better, brighter, harder working, more seasoned staff. Productivity soars. The return on investment is huge."

A RETURN TO THE DELTA

As we close, I'll invite you one last time to think about the images I presented you with on the first page of chapter 1. In one set of images, we have a dumpy old office. And in the other set, we have modern, inspiring, cutting-edge space. We've discussed many benefits that come from choosing Building B—better recruiting, retention, and engagement; differentiate your company from the competition; enhance your culture and brand; and on and on—but ultimately, the most compelling reason to do this is that it isn't even a blip on the operating budget.

What we're looking at is the delta. When considering your next office space, always keep in mind that you're never going to find a rent that is $0 per square foot. No matter where you wind up, that cost is likely to check in around 3% to 7% of your total operating budget. So if we're imagining that premium space will lead to a 20% increase in that 3% to 7% expense, we're not talking about a huge rent hike here. We're talking about pennies on the dollar of an investment that leads to dollars on the penny of productivity increases. Or, as Jamie Rogers put it, "This is an expense either way. But it's really just an incremental increase between outdated office space and this great new stuff."

For a company occupying a space roughly the size of Rice Energy, we're talking about maybe a five-dollar-per-square-foot increase in rent. Even if the spaces are massive—and even if you're making them larger by adding 15,000 square feet of shared space—it's still just a drop in the bucket compared to the average general and administrative expense budget. "Proportionally, it's not a lot of money," Jamie said. "It's nothing compared to payroll. Our move wound up costing about one half of one percent of our total payroll expenses, and now we have this space that everyone can enjoy on a daily basis. Look, I'm a numbers guy, and these numbers just make sense any way you look at them."

CONCLUSION

YOUR FUTURE IS BRIGHT (AND ALSO MOBILE, AGILE, AND FLEXIBLE)

"Be all in or get all out. There is no halfway."
- Anonymous

Think about the first time you went to the ballpark when you were a kid. If you were from Pittsburgh, that might have happened at Three Rivers Stadium, or depending on your age, even at Forbes Field. A trip like that didn't cost nearly as much back then as it does now, and the experience was about one thing: watching a baseball game. When you were a kid, maybe it was also about getting a hot dog and a soda and some ice cream, but apart from that, you had your seat and the game happening on the field.

The situation is a little different today at PNC Park (and at any other new stadium in every American sport, for that matter). These facilities went from just housing a game and selling some tickets and low-level concessions to selling *experiences*. There are few modern stadiums that don't offer gourmet restaurants, fancy bars, luxury suites, and entertainment for the kids.

The reason is simple: modern culture has become experience-driven. When given the choice between a no-frills ballpark and a place where you can enjoy a five-star meal, take a few hacks in the batting cages, and then kick back in your plush seat to take in some of the game, you're picking the second option every time. The pull is so compelling that they even tore down venerable Yankee Stadium to create a modern version with all the luxuries. Even Wrigley and Fenway have undergone multi-million-dollar renovations to keep up with the demand for experiential trips to the ballpark.

Think of the work your company does as that baseball game. It has to happen. It's why you exist as an organization. Think of your people as the players and coaches that play the game. Without them, the work

---

Photo: The Riviera – Architectural design by NEXT Architecture.

doesn't happen—and if they're uninspired by the facilities, their work is likely to suffer. Think of your customers as the fans that occupy the stadium. They're going to judge who you are as an organization based on the quality of the venue you provide for your staff (and for your customers themselves) to occupy.

If you ignore this push toward experience-driven facilities, then you send the wrong message to your players, to your leaders, and to your fans, and you wind up languishing in mediocrity—or worse, getting blown away by a competitor who got ahead of the trend, disrupted your industry, and moved to a dynamic office space while you were still stuck in neutral.

DON'T GET RUN OVER BY SOMEONE ELSE'S RPMS

The truth is that it's only a matter of time before someone in your industry makes this leap. Very soon, generational drift will translate to significant turnover in the decision-making chairs in every industry. And I can tell you from experience that every new CEO comes in and wants to put his or her stamp on the culture of the company he or she is running. More and more people who attend CEO summits are saying, "We absolutely need to upgrade to a better office space." They aren't saying this because they just *love* the idea of spending more money. They're saying this because they recognize the essential benefits that come with better vibe, enhanced experience, and luxurious amenities.

In an era when people are expected to be available after work and on weekends; in an era where absenteeism and turnover are such huge and costly problems; and in an era when 70% of American employees feel disengaged at work, why would you not want to do something to re-engage your people? You're never going to hear someone argue that raising employee engagement is a bad thing, and yet some decision-makers still want to avoid paying slightly more for their rent.

I've said it many times over the course of this book, but keep in mind that for almost every company in every industry, rent typically represents somewhere between 3% and 7% of the overall operating budget. In other words, we're talking about one of your least significant line items. If increasing that small line item by a few thousand dollars a year is going to lead to hundreds of thousands or even millions of dollars in savings on recruitment, retention, and productivity, then why would you keep your people slogging through their work in an outdated space? Why not invest in something that will have an enormous impact on what is likely your biggest line item, the one that allocates 50% to 65% of your operating budget to payroll and payroll-related expenses?

When I'm trying to cut expenses at my business, I go to my big line-items first, and I'm sure I'm not alone in that tendency. Worrying about the rent, meanwhile, is pennywise and pound foolish—especially since even a small increase in what you're paying can drastically cut down on disengagement and improve productivity across the board.

Some of the decision-makers who ignore this competitive advantage (because of the mistaken assumption that it costs too much) will simply ignore the need to improve engagement and reduce employee turnover and absenteeism. Those decision-makers are going to be in for a rough run as the talent war continues to heat up. Others will attempt different strategies like offering higher salaries or better benefits packages. But raising salaries, offering bonuses, and improving benefits costs money, too—in fact, it costs many multiples more than the increased rent in a dynamic office space, and in almost every case, the boost to productivity is much less pronounced or lasting.

Sure, giving someone a raise will make them happier with their jobs in the short term, but that feeling wears off as soon as their lifestyles and expenses rise to the level of their new salaries. Giving them a better title is great, right up until that title becomes just another part of their identity, something assumed and taken for granted. Eventually, they start looking to move to another employer offering the same or better title, salary, and benefits. Then you're stuck holding the bag on the staggering costs of searching for a replacement and training that replacement. Plus, the replacement isn't likely to be as good at the job as the one you lost (at least not for the first year or two). Even in the cases where you find someone who can replicate that productivity, it always takes a long time for them to get up to speed. And every day they spend at something less than full capacity is a day that costs you money.

Times have changed. More and more employees from every generation are focused on their work-life blend, and when you have so many people trying to find ways to be happy *now,* it's shocking how little money and titles matter when compared to their day to day experience. Conversely, if you take the steps necessary to improve your staff's day to day experience, and you give them something tangible—something great that they can see and interact with and be inspired by every day—then the effects are long-lasting, considerable, and extend across the board to *every* member of your staff.

In a world where we never turn off work or turn off life, the answer is to give your people a place where they all *want to be*. An inspiring place. A place where they can exercise, eat healthy, and actually enjoy being. A place where they can work in natural light, breathe fresh air, be happy, and share positive experiences with their coworkers. A place where they don't mind sticking around into the evening hours when the situation calls for it. A place where work-life blend truly exists and is celebrated in a way that lowers stress, improves wellbeing, and allows your staff to work at their highest level.

THE EVOLUTION TO A *BRIGHTER* FUTURE

Given the pace of technological, demographic, and cultural changes, the evolution of office space has been rapid (and the changes will only speed up as the talent war peaks). In the years to come, we're going to see many and more new, progressive ideas that will change the way we think about corporate space and culture. To keep pace with this evolution, it's important to remain agile, mobile, and flexible, but at the start, it also helps to see what we're evolving toward.

If you want to know what the future of office space looks like, just take a look at the rendering at the start of this chapter. That's the Riviera, our newest project at Burns Scalo. It features everything that occupiers are going to both want and *need* in the coming years, as they engage with the heightening talent war and try to get the best out of their people.

First, the building is close to restaurants, hotels, great housing, and several major universities. Inside, it features a lobby with a concierge desk; a fitness center with separate steam rooms in the men's and women's locker rooms; an outdoor deck that overlooks the river; a rack of bicycles available on demand for employees and guests to use on the nearby biking and jogging trail; a shuttle service to nearby amenities; leisure and gaming facilities; and enough scalability and adaptability to meet almost any company's evolving demands.

The first floor serves as something of an incubator or coworking space, a place for every employee of every business in the building to congregate, meet, and collaborate. It has the floors for conventional offices with dynamic workspaces, huddle and phone rooms, buzzworthy conference rooms, and flexible technology with extraordinary WiFi, a media wall brings messaging and movement to the lobby, click-share, remote accessibility, and AI integration everywhere you turn. There are also the more social meeting spaces like the cafés and the rooftop terrace.

Like the offices of the future, tenants at the Riviera can design their spaces around a need for flexibility and mobility. Some companies prefer unassigned seats, where their people can occupy one workspace one day and another the next. Some feature the mix of traditional desks and sit-stand workspaces, fully open and collaborative spaces alongside rooms that accommodate private conversation and head-down work. Some will dedicate space solely to workspace while others will design creative spaces meant for collaboration, brainstorming, and innovation. Some will want to take advantage of the integrated speakers that allow them to play music throughout the space they occupy, an effort that heightens the mood, keeps people engaged and energized, and serves as a nice conversation piece with visiting customers, prospects, and partners.

In short, the Riviera brings the luxury hotel vibe. It isn't an office, it's a *destination*—an engaging, enjoyable, cool place where recruits, employees, and customers will *want* to be. It's the kind of location that delivers on all the latest amenities, where anyone present can have more of their daily needs met while in the office, and where anyone who works there can be proud to share their experience with friends, family, and professional connections.

This is where the workplace is evolving: *brighter* lights inside the building, *brighter* people recruited into the company, *brighter* ideas, and a *brighter* future, as a result.

BE AGILE, MOBILE, AND FLEXIBLE

Think about your last new car. Recall that feeling you had when you first took it for a test drive. Why is that feeling so warm? It's because upgrading from an old car to a new one—or an old anything to a new anything—is *rewarding.* It's *satisfying* to have something new and better. You enjoy the new luxury on a whole different level. And you appreciate it more too. How many times have you bought a new car and then swore you would never allow yourself or any of your passengers to eat in it? Of course no one ever sticks to that vow for longer than a few weeks, but it always comes from the same place: the vibe of having that new car is just so *enjoyable*. It is the kind of vibe that, at least for a while, enhances your feelings about the rest of your life.

So as you entertain a move to a new office space, it's important to leave room for change, and more importantly, for *upgrades*. Even small upgrades, provided that those upgrades contribute to your sense of wellbeing, can make a huge difference. Why do you think those lines get so long at every Apple Store in America every time a new iPhone is released? Upgrading is an incredible feeling.

The best part is that these upgrades and their accompanying vibes don't have to happen just once and then you're done. You can upgrade as often as people improve their homes, buy or lease a new car, or even get a new iPhone. Your space shouldn't be a static entity, but rather, something that remains agile, flexible, and mobile through consistent upgrades. Think about how often consumer televisions upgrade. It wasn't long ago that people were excited about digital cable. Then it was HD. Then companies started playing around with 3-D and Ultra-HD. Now it's 4k. Every couple of years, a new technology emerges to make new TVs completely mind-blowing compared to the once-mind-blowing TVs they're replacing.

When it comes to technology, nothing is static. Everything changes and evolves, and each new change arrives quicker than the last. So as you consider your opportunity for upgrades to the physical space, new technology is an obvious place to start, but the bottom line is that you should be willing to adapt, update, and improve anything in the office that isn't bolted to the floor (or in other words, almost everything).

Don't forget the music, either. Some employers will pipe in the same music every week and never change it. That can *really* impact morale. Sometimes, keeping things fresh is simply a matter of rotating the music regularly.

There is nothing worse than a stagnant space. Likewise, there are few greater drags on culture and employee productivity than an element of the space that everyone, or even just a key employee, doesn't like. Enhancing the space helps keep things fresh, and soliciting employee input on *how* to enhance that space only furthers the message that leadership cares. Every time you upgrade, you don't just send those positive vibes about the newness and better-ness of the upgrade; you also send one more reaffirming message that you are invested in your people's comfort, happiness, and success. This message leads to better culture, better retention, and it *absolutely* resonates with recruits.

On the mobility front, the future is all about choice. The choice to work remotely once in a while. The choice to put in your work during nontraditional working hours. The choice to work for an hour at your designated space, an hour in the café, and an hour in a huddle room before taking a break to grab a healthy lunch and use the fitness center. This mobility helps smooth out the demands of modern work by offering outlets to reenergize by changing the environment, exercising, or even blowing off a little steam with a competitive game or a social gathering. No matter who you are, you're going to prefer brighter spaces, higher ceilings, more and bigger windows, engaging music, good food, a place to exercise, and the opportunity to interact with your coworkers—and those opportunities will show up in your work product and productivity.

The final piece, flexibility, is all about making room for your company and its people to grow and change over time. Smart buildings allow for a company to grow with technological change. Flexible spaces recognize that people and their employers have individual preferences and behaviors. Flexible furniture systems allow employees to change from sitting to standing, partitioned to fully open, or even work while exercising.

The call for flexibility also recognizes that as people age, they value different things, and so the amenities and services you offer must be flexible enough to meet those different demands. If we polled everyone at Burns Scalo—and we have staff members from four generations (Boomers, Generation X, Millennials, and Generation Z)—about what they appreciate most about our company, everyone would give a wildly different answer based on age.

The employees closer to retirement (Boomers) would probably list the healthcare or the 401(k) matching. The ones who are just starting families favor the life insurance or flexible schedule. The Millennials and Gen Zers are probably interested in the free phone and data plan. But you know what? When they get older, they'll start liking the life insurance and healthcare and 401(k) matching even while they continue to appreciate the phone. Meanwhile, *everyone,* no matter what their generation, is going to like half-day Fridays and the fitness center (even if they don't take advantage of either).

SOCIETY IS ALWAYS MOVING FORWARD

Even now, after all these pages on the positive effects of dynamic office space, you might be thinking, *Yeah, this Jim guy is making sense, but there's no reason to do this now.* Whatever year it is when you pick up this book, there's a chance that 2030 still feels like a long way off. You might be thinking, *I'll get to this eventually. Right now, though, we just have too much going on.* Or maybe you're thinking you'll wait until the "time is right," whenever that might be. Let me tell you, the time is now. Society is always moving forward. You can't afford to avoid moving with it. The time to start moving with it is now, especially considering that, depending on the size of your company, the actual move can take one to two years.

I recently read an article about estate planning that made this great point: "It's always better to be a year too early than a year too late." And I had a life insurance salesman say to me once, "You don't need life insurance. Just don't die." If we apply those lessons to office space, then it's clear that there's no way to know exactly when these technological, cultural, professional, and societal changes are going to run you over and make your business irrelevant. So why wait around to find out?

This is a fact: businesses across every industry are already making this change. By way of the biggest example, take retail giant Amazon. At the time of this writing, Amazon has decided to open a second headquarters. Not only is the decision to open a second headquarters disruptive, but so is the process they're undertaking to choose the city where they'll set up shop in the new space. They've narrowed the choice down to one of twenty finalist cities, and the simple act of doing this has totally disrupted the way people think about office space.

We'll see where Amazon lands—and soon after, we'll see exactly *how* they use that unprecedented second-and-equal HQ—but it's my theory that they're following this plan because they feel like they've exhausted the labor market in the Pacific Northwest, and want to open themselves up to a new pool of talent in the much more populous east coast. Further, if they open their second HQ on the east coast, then they can say to any recruit, "Where do you want to work? East coast? West coast? You pick." Further, when that recruit becomes a new hire, that new hire can take comfort in the knowledge that, if someday their life or their preferences call them to the other coast, they can move basically at will.

This, of course, is my opinion. We will see how it shakes out. But until we learn the truth, the fact remains that Amazon's efforts represent a disruptive shift. This one company, almost by itself, is changing the way we all think about the power of where you choose to house your business.

And every other business is only going to follow their lead. If you don't yet have a competitor who occupies a dynamic office space, you will have one soon. As every element of society and culture moves toward vibe and experience, we must move along with it, or we risk getting left behind. By 2025, 70% of the workforce will be from the Millennial and Gen Z generations. By 2030, the numbers will only get more drastic. If you're not in position to give this huge chunk of the workforce what they want, they will be far less likely to choose to work for you. That's true *today,* and it will only get truer with every passing year.

As decision-makers, we can't ignore this anymore. Great spaces and great cultures are all around us. Hotels, restaurants, airports, ballparks—they're all pivoting toward luxury and experience. This is becoming the new reality, one where you can't put your people in a bad space and expect to have a great culture and a great outcome.

So as you consider the next place to house your company, remember that there's always cheaper space. You can always find somewhere with lower rent. But a dynamic space is not comparable to a place that can give you the best *deal* on the rent. It's like trying to compare a Cadillac to a Chevy. Same automaker, totally different car. One offers luxury and the other affordability—and the way people react to them could not be more different. Price is just one piece of the value proposition, and if you're trying to stay relevant into the future, it's one of the less important pieces. While modern culture continues its shift toward luxury and experience, you still can't have champagne taste on a beer budget.

The future of office space is about a lot of things, but from your chair, it's all going to boil down to the same thing: pay more, get more. Recognize that word "value" in "value proposition." Pay more for relative value and that relative value will pay you back in spades.

Rent it and they will come. I can say this because the data is overwhelmingly in favor of it, but at the end of the day, what does the data matter compared to the more tangible results? I can tell you firsthand that all the best and brightest companies we have worked with over the years at Burns Scalo, all those companies that have already gone through this experience of upgrading to dynamic office space—as painful and expensive as it can seem sometimes—have enjoyed immediate payback in terms of productivity from day one. In every case, that productivity has led to these new spaces completely paying for themselves inside the first three years.

On top of that, the leaders of all these companies will tell you that once you make this move, you'll never want to go back. If we left the Bentley for one of our previous offices, there would be an immediate and overwhelming productivity dump. Once you raise your standards, you never want to lower them again.

I'll finish the way I started. All businesses are about two things: people and money. If we focus on those two key elements, people and money, then no matter what the future brings, it will always be bright. If we take care of our people, it might cost a little more, but the returns on those investments will more than make up for it. Make this leap and you will never look back. You will stay relevant. You will grow as an organization. You will win the talent war. And ten years from now, you will still find yourself in an inviting, inspiring, engaging space full of happy people who enjoy working for you, working with each other, and working to *life*.